BILL BRYANT SR.

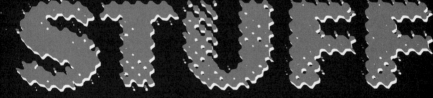

STRICTLY STREET STUFF

A STREETWISE GUIDE TO PERSONAL PROTECTION

PALADIN PRESS
BOULDER, COLORADO

Strictly Street Stuff:
A Streetwise Guide to Personal Protection
by Bill Bryant Sr.

Copyright © 2005 by Bill Bryant Sr.

ISBN 10: 1-58160-481-5
ISBN 13: 978-1-58160-481-8
Printed in the United States of America

Published by Paladin Press, a division of
Paladin Enterprises, Inc.,
Gunbarrel Tech Center
7077 Winchester Circle
Boulder, Colorado 80301 USA
+1.303.443.7250

Direct inquiries and/or orders to the above address.

Visit our Web site at www.paladin-press.com

Table of Contents

Introduction 1

Mind-Set
The Street Fight
Selecting a School
A Note on Clothing

Chapter 1: The Basics 9

Fighting Stance
Punches
Kicks
Heel Tactics
Throws
Footwork

Chapter 2: Breakaways. 31

Wrist Grabs
Lapel Grabs
Rear Shoulder Grabs
Full Nelson
Headlock
Front Two-Hand Choke
Rear Naked Choke
Bear Hug
Hammer Lock

Chapter 3: Defending against Various Blows and Throws 49

Takedowns
Kicks
Punches

Chapter 4: Preemptive Attacks. 57

Chapter 5: Ground Grappling 59

You Are in His Guard
You Have Mounted
You Are in His Mount
He Is in Your Guard
He Is Standing, and You Are Down
He Has You in a Rear Scissors Hold
He Has You in a Headlock
Get Up!

Chapter 6: Weapons. 83

Handguns
He Has a Gun (Oh, No!)
Knives
Weapons at Hand
Your Mind

Chapter 7: Physical Training 119

Loosening Up
Circuit Training
Stretching
The Final Exercises

Chapter 8: Personalized Combat Form. 133

Epilogue. 139

Warning

he information contained in this book can be dangerous and could result in serious injury or death. It is the reader's responsibility to research and comply with all laws regarding self-defense, justified use of force in defense of one's life, and related areas. The author, publisher, and distributors of this book disclaim any liability from any damage or injuries of any type that a reader or user of information contained in this book may incur from the use or misuse of said information. This book is presented for *academic study only.*

Consult with a qualified medical practitioner to establish your health and fitness capacity before embarking on any physical training program.

Preface

his book is not normal. It is about brawling, and although martial arts are mentioned, they are neither glamorized nor vilified. What I want you to know is that the price you paid for this book will be money well spent. My intent was to produce a book that virtually anyone could use to improve his or her chances of surviving a violent encounter. I also wanted to entertain instead of making it one of those dry books on how to deliver a rear snake fang kick to the left nostril of Godzilla.

Read it over and over, learn what is offered, modify it if you need to, and make it your own. Enjoy the tales of brawls, but keep in mind that the reality of close-quarter combat is not entertaining; it is horrid. People get hurt—sometimes seriously, permanently, or fatally. Train hard, and pass this information on to folks who will use it wisely.

Acknowledgments

would like to thank my wife, Addie; my son Bill; Wayne "Scrapper" Fisher (www.train-forstrength.com); and Paladin editorial director Jon Ford of Paladin Press, who pushed me to get *Strictly Street Stuff* into print. Without their encouragement, it just wouldn't have happened. I would also like to thank Paladin editor Karen Petersen for her commitment to this project, Jeremy Stalnecker for his photographic skill, and Ryan Gass, who suffered valiantly as we posed for the photos.

Introduction

uring the time it will take you to read this small book, literally hundreds of violent crimes will have occurred in the United States. Thousands of martial arts schools flourish in this country. Millions of people practice these arts in the hope that they can gain some small amount of control over the violence that confronts us all daily, yet many are unsure that their knowledge will prove effective if they are required to use it. Millions more live in fear of physical violence but do not have the opportunity to learn an effective form of self-defense. This book is intended to help those who practice any of the various forms of self-defense, as well as those who try to learn without the benefit of an experienced trainer.

The object of this whole book is to get folks to develop and train with a series of techniques that they will practice over and over until the techniques become as natural as walking. Simply put, *you will do what you train to do*. If you don't train, you will do what comes naturally, and that may or may not be the best thing to do.

I have practiced a wide variety of martial

arts and brawled my way through many of the world's major ports, learning the hard way what works and what doesn't through violent confrontations in barrooms and back alleys. Working as a shore patrolman for the U.S. Navy and as a doorman/bouncer for a security company reinforced what I had learned during my wilder boozing days.

That information was simple, and it is what I intend to pass on here: low kicks and knees; simple, tripping-type throws; four specific punches; some grappling; and a mélange of dirty tricks. Those few techniques combined with good physical conditioning and a will-win mental attitude will usually carry the day. Keep in mind that on any given day *anybody* can be beaten. Who was the wise man who said, "There was never a horse that couldn't be rode, and never a cowboy that couldn't be throwed"?

MIND-SET

I knew the man. He was a former heavyweight boxer who was six inches taller than I and outweighed me by over 100 pounds. He sucker-punched me with a straight right when I walked over to him at the locker club. I had been hit before, knocked out even, but that one just about took my head off without putting me out. When I finished ricocheting off of lockers and benches and got my feet back under me, he was headed my way. That is when I made one of the dumbest statements of my life: "I'm gonna whip your butt."

If I landed any punches, he never seemed to notice. I never felt anything either. Fueled by a towering rage, I attempted to punch my way out of a senseless situation. We fought our way across the second floor, and he knocked me down the stairs and into the lobby. We fought our way across the lobby, through the door, and out onto the sidewalk, where he continued to wail on me and then suddenly just dropped like a stone. To this day I believe that he had been drinking, and the combination of booze and the exertion of beating on me caused him to pass out. I'm sure it wasn't one of my punches.

Two guys came out and dragged him inside as I stood there and took stock of my situation. I had lost both shoes, one sock, and my shirt, but I had gained a collection of scratches and dirt, an eye that was quickly swelling shut, and a split lip. I would wake up the next morning feeling like I had been left in a commercial clothes dryer that had been turned on high.

I won that fight because I never quit, not because I was stronger or more skilled at fighting.

When it comes to mind-set, train yourself to adhere to the following principles:

1) Number one is *believe in yourself.* If your opponent is bigger than you are, then you are faster and more agile. If he is more skillful, then you are more vicious. If he is younger, then you are more stable and experienced. *Always believe you have an advantage.*

2) Number two is *mentally prepare to react with a fighting rage when attacked.* Every time you feel pain, react with anger, not apathy. Every time you feel fear, react with anger. All of that high-minded crud about "total control," "mind of no mind," and so forth is just that— crud. Some true sociopaths are able to commit total mayhem and not even get their pulse rate up. They may be able to fight and not really feel any emotion to speak of. The rest of us are going to feel something, and if you intend to win, it had better be anger, even rage. Most good street fighters have the ability to turn on instant rage. I use this mantra when I am jumping rope

and at other times when I am doing some mindless, repetitive, task: *"Any time I attack or am attacked, I go into a fighting rage/my fear turns into a fighting rage/my pain turns into a fighting rage/attack the joints, genitals, neck, and eyes/use a weapon."* Tell yourself this over and over again, and it will become a part of your mental makeup that will come roaring out when the fit hits the shan.

3) Number three is *always be aware of your surroundings.* If you walk into a place and have that feeling that there is something wrong, don't shrug it off and go about your business—get the heck out of there! Your subconscious is simply a lot smarter than you are when it comes to sensing danger. Do not be afraid to be inconvenienced.

If you are in a verbal conflict with a possible attacker, never obey his commands even if he is armed; he will try to move you to someplace else so he can do more damage without being interrupted.

Every time you go into a place, catalog the exits, survey for usable weapons, and notice what the other occupants are doing. By *place* I mean anywhere—a parking lot is a place, the walkway up to your home is a place; you get the picture. I am not trying to say always be in condition red with your hand on a Smith & Wesson. What I am saying is, pay attention to everything that is going on around you; the time you spend in la-la land is the time you are most likely to get hurt.

THE STREET FIGHT

Keep in mind that there are actually very few knockouts in a street fight. Usually, the fight ends when there is a beat-down that doesn't involve a knockout, or a bystander stops the fight, or one of the brawlers sprints away from the scene. Herein lies one of the most important lessons of this book. *The sprint works virtually every time, even against weapons.* You have been practicing leaping away from dangerous things and running like crazy ever since you were a kid. This is the win-win technique for any confrontation because no one gets hurt. On the other hand, if some slob is groping your girlfriend and you choose to use the sprint, you may live to regret it. You will read the word *sprint* over and over again throughout this book; I've used it a few times, and I've wished I had even more times.

Also keep in mind that whenever you fight, you face a lot of unseen dangers. The opponent's friends and relatives can suddenly spring into action and change the course of your life.

I was watching a friend of mine do the ground-and-pound on one of his enemies in the other guy's front yard one time, when suddenly, the guy's father came leaping off the porch and started slamming a coke bottle into the back of my friend's head. Of course, we put a stop to that, but it didn't change the fact that my friend needed stitches and had to change his jeans.

Policemen in some areas often use the rear naked choke to subdue violent suspects, but keep in mind that they have backup and even then are in great danger because they are trying to subdue someone without actually damaging him or her. In the world of street fighting, any time you tie up both of your hands, as in a rear naked choke, your opponent has one or both hands free and can pull a knife and cut you severely before you can choke him out. Twice I have been kicked in the head by bystanders when I had someone on the ground and was in the process of choking him out. I finally decided that hold belongs in the dojo, not in the street.

Your first response should always be to flee the scene, get the heck out of Dodge, cover 'em up with heel dust, or any other phrase that gets across the idea of running for your life. *No one wins a fight; there are just different degrees of losing.* If you have no choice but to fight, then your objective should be to stop your opponent long enough for you to escape. There are no rules, there are no rules, there are no rules—do what it takes to end the assault. This may mean striking the first blow, it may mean using weapons, and it may mean doing things that will leave lasting injuries. If you weren't allowed to escape, that was because your attacker believed he/she had a distinct advantage and was going to be able to control and injure you. To avoid allowing that to happen, you must, for a few moments, become the most savage animal on the face of the earth.

SELECTING A SCHOOL

As I look back over my last 55 years of studying and practicing a variety of martial arts, competing in tournaments, brawling in bars and back alleys around the world, and discussing the fine art of personal conflict with hundreds of folks who have been there, I can see many of the pros and cons of commerce in personal combat arts.

Had I not been beaten on a regular basis when I was a kid, I might have been more afraid to engage in fisticuffs. I learned early on that you can live through pain, be motivated by it, endure, and overcome. I paid no money for that lesson, but it was perhaps my most valuable.

I learned from my late brother to close the gap, clinch, use tripping throws, ground and pound, apply pressure points for pain to break holds, and apply the rear naked choke. Again, this cost nothing in the way of money, but I paid a price in pain.

Playing judo with navy clubs reinforced my belief that tripping throws are useful in the street and that other, more spectacular types of throws can be hazardous to your health. It cost me absolutely nothing but the price of a gi. It also taught me that competing against people who want to hurt you (judo is not "the gentle art") is the best way to train for violent personal conflict.

I learned kali, Western boxing, jun fan kickboxing, and

various forms of jiu-jitsu and karate from a variety of sources. Each art had something valuable, but many had the inevitable bovine excrement thrown into the mix. When an instructor gives you a rap about being able to defeat anyone, how lethal he is, and so on, just know that this person is going to be lethal to your wallet if you fall for it.

I recommend that you find a school that emphasizes fitness, cross-training, and competition under conditions that are as realistic as possible. Training is fine, and sparring is even better because it helps you develop skills that can't be taught other than through experience. An even more valuable experience is to engage in violent personal conflict with someone who wants to throw you down and/or knock you out. This is why I believe competition, especially in a mixed martial arts setting, is so important. This controlled competition is about as close as you are going to get to the real thing, and you don't want to engage in the real thing except as a last resort. Keep in mind that any violent sport has an element of danger and that even ones that are not combat-related are a useful training ground. Wrestling, boxing, judo, and such are excellent training arenas, but so are football, hockey, water polo, and other contact sports. They all help develop the mind-set that is needed in a violent personal conflict.

No matter what kind of school you practice in, I strongly recommend that you practice alone as well. Develop your own training area that most closely resembles places where you are most likely to have to defend yourself. Make sure that there is sometimes junk on the floor that you have to maneuver around and can pick up and use for weapons. This is a good place for your own homemade grappling dummy, various punching bags, and weapons that you think might be available.

Get to where you enjoy this solo training; it may be among the most valuable training tools you have at your disposal.

A NOTE ON CLOTHING

Needless to say, you should regularly train in the clothes that you are likely to be wearing when you get in a scrap. I have never yet seen anyone get in a street fight wearing any kind of kimono, gi, or such. Wear the type of clothing you are likely to be wearing when you fight. If you normally wear a business suit, buy one at a thrift store and practice in that so you can discover the strengths and limitations of what you typically wear.

Billy Jack taking off his boots to kick someone in that scene from *The Trial of Billy Jack* was ridiculous. Your feet will be a lot slower and less nimble when you are wearing boots instead of sneakers, but boots can be a formidable weapon if used properly (high kicks are not among the proper uses). Wear shoes that have some form of stiffened sole, such as dress, court, or skate shoes. Jogging shoes are fine for jogging but provide little protection to the toes in the event of a fight.

Jeans provide more protection against a knife than any other standard clothing I know of. Leather chaps and the chain saw or double-ply jeans many loggers and outdoor workers wear are better, of course, but don't qualify as standard. Because of their tightness and thickness, jeans also protect you from groin grabs to a large extent.

Even in warm weather, it is good to have a jacket and cap at hand to use for throwing and blocking. A cap or hat (or anything else) thrown into the face of an attacker will gain you a moment's distraction and allow you to recover and either make your getaway or launch an attack.

The Basics

hese "basics" consist of the physical how-to, or mechanics, of techniques that are used over and over throughout this book. In a fight, they often chain together to form combinations that continue to evolve until the incident is over. It isn't over until you are safe—that is, the person who attacked you is unable to continue and/or you have managed to escape the area. These basic techniques include your fighting stance, punching, kicking, heel tactics, throws, and footwork. Other techniques will be described in the book, but those described in this chapter are used over and over again to respond to a variety of situations and should be practiced until they are as natural as walking.

FIGHTING STANCE

This is the standing position that you would normally adopt for fighting. Your feet are slightly spread, and the foot corresponding to your lead hand is approximately 15 inches in front of the rear foot. The rear heel is kept slightly raised most of the time. Your forearms should be almost straight up, and the knuckles aligned with and about 4 inches away from your cheekbones in a "high guard" position. When you are sparring you can launch almost any striking attack from this position. In a fight you will often recover to this position momentarily before launching a counterattack.

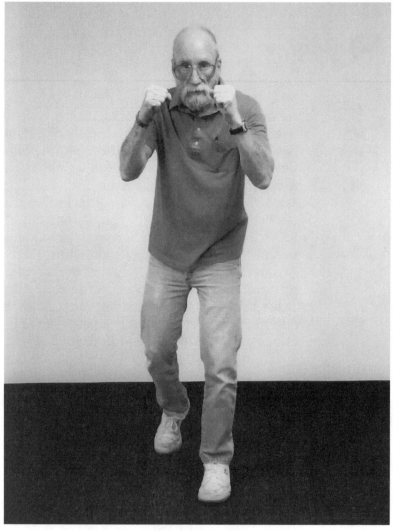

Fighting stance.

PUNCHES

I was half-crocked and acting pretty rowdy in a bar in Honolulu when a guy who passed himself off as the manager came up and told me that I was causing too much of a disturbance and should go outside for a while to calm down. I knew he was right, and I had just been having some "innocent" fun, so I went along with his suggestion and walked out the back door of the joint with him. As we stood there in the alley I decided to light up a cigarette. Since we were facing each other while we shot the breeze, I twisted my body to the right to keep from flashing the lighter in his face. Unfortunately for him, he launched a belly bomb as I twisted away, and it merely grazed across my gut. I was already in the wound-up position, my hands near my face, left lead, balanced—he never even got his hand back before my right hand, filled with cigarette lighter, rocketed into his chin. It was a perfect straight right. He stumbled back a couple of steps, hit the wall, slid down, and stayed there.

When developing your punches, assume the fighting stance and then imagine that your body is a two-by-four, mounted vertically, with a steel rod running through the middle of it lengthwise. The end of the steel rod is directly between your feet. As you punch, use your legs to spin the two-by-four. When the two-by-four covers about half of its 90-degree spin, the arm and shoulder drive the punch into and through the target. The nonhitting hand will almost always be kept in or drawn to the high guard. By raising the lead foot slightly off the ground as you drive the punch forward, you increase power by putting your weight into the punch; however, this is a total commitment and should be practiced until it is as natural as walking before it is ever attempted.

- *The Palm Heel Thrust* (PHT) mainly targets the nose and jaw but is useful anywhere on the head because it delivers full force and does not skip off as readily as the knuckles. You are a lot less likely to break your hand when using this blow, but it really only seems to work well for the first strike in a combination. It can be delivered with full power without being in the fighting stance, making it an ideal first strike. Don't believe that old tale about it breaking the nose bone and driving it into someone's brain; the nose is mostly cartilage, and there is a lot of sinus between the nose and brain, you will definitely hurt someone with a PHT to the nose, but you aren't likely to kill him. When your hands are open and held somewhat low or away from your centerline, you can drive in the PHT with considerable force from wherever it is without telegraphing the punch as much as you would if you clenched your fist. You should follow a less-than-solid hit with the PHT by sliding your thumb across your opponent's eye, blur-

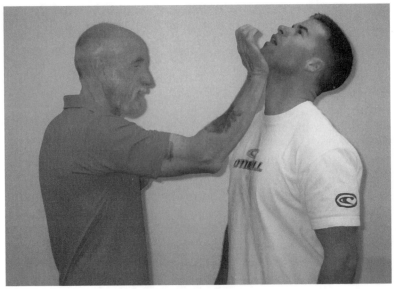

Palm heel thrust (PHT).

ring his vision, and even continuing on to grasp the rear of his head and pull it toward you as you head-butt his face.

- *The Jab* mainly just targets the nose and eyes. It is delivered with your hand(s) closed or closing and originates from your centerline or from the high guard position. It is up in the line of your opponent's vision, but with practice it is blur-fast. It can either be worked in the vertical fist position or with the fist rotating to the horizontal position as it is shot forward. Practice both types of jabs. The jab is always delivered with the lead hand and is usually delivered as the first strike in a combination or as one of a series of jabs that are disruptive, exploratory strikes that set up some other technique. With practice the jab may have enough power to actually end the fight.
- *The Straight Punch* is the number-two in most combinations and targets the throat. (If you don't hit the throat, you will probably hit the jaw, which is almost as good.)

Jab.

It is the second in your combination because it is hard to throw the straight punch with much power unless you can get your hands up and at least partially closed. Getting the hands up telegraphs your intentions, so it is not likely to be your lead punch unless you have already adopted a fighting stance with your hands up. Even then it is a secondary type of lead, because you would mainly lead with the jab when sparring.

The book *Minimizing Reflex and Reaction Time* by the American Sports Research Association (sold through Health for Life) states that the effect of your first strike (whether it lands or not) gives you about a half-second window of opportunity to land the second blow before your opponent can react. In that half-second, you want to take away his ability to breathe well or even knock him out with that straight punch to the throat.

- *The Bottom Fist Strike* targets anyplace on the head. It is delivered with the little-finger side of your fist as you

Straight punch.

are turning to face an opponent. You may not always be able to strike the target, but you will have a hand up to deflect incoming blows and will be giving yourself that half-second window for the second strike. Another time it is useful is when your attacker bends forward and you can chop down to the back of his head with the bottom fist. That bend over is usually due to a kick to the family jewels, but I have also had people bend over like that after they took a couple of solid shots to the face.

- *The Forearm Blow* uses virtually the same mechanics as a punch when you are standing; it is just thrown from a shorter range when you are using the little-finger side of your forearm. Using the thumb side of the forearm is a bit different. You need to be low and slightly to the side of your opponent and then whip that forearm and fist up and into his groin.

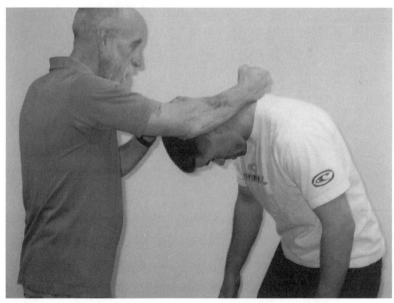

Bottom fist strike.

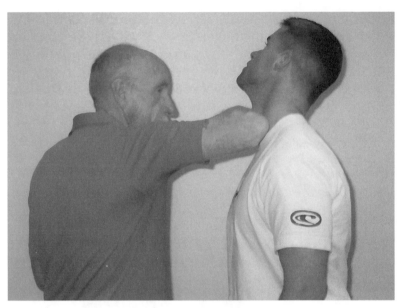

Forearm, little-finger side.

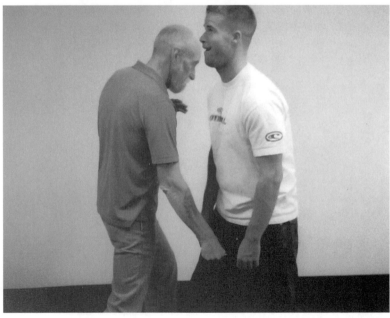

Forearm, thumb side.

KICKS

In Marseille, France, Penny was in some sort of an argument with a Frenchman near the waterfront when things turned nasty. Suddenly the Frenchman's foot grazed the side of Penny's cheek. Penny covered up and started hooking and jabbing when the foot flashed by his face again. He tried the only kick he knew, straight from the ground to the groin. He followed with a hard right hook, and we ran for the ship as the foot fighter became acquainted with the ground.

Simply put, kicking is not all it is cracked up to be. There are experts out there who can do fabulous stuff, but if you are not an expert kicker, leave those feet on the ground where they can hold you up.

- *Front Kick.* This is used for a distraction when fired toward the shin and for business when delivered so the instep and/or ankle are driven into the opponent's groin. Practice using both the lead and rear legs for this

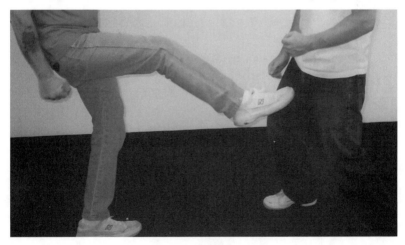

Front kick.

Knee, preparation.   **Knee, strike.**

kick, and use the natural motion that you would when punting a football. Don't worry about pointing the knee, driving with your hips, and all that other power-kick stuff. You want to get it into the target and back on the ground before it gets caught. Practice it standing still, moving around in your fighting stance, and walking toward someone normally.

- *Knee.* This is one of the cornerstone techniques of infighting. Practice slamming that knee into the thighs, groin, and abdomen of your opponent. Start with your kneeing foot stretched out behind you and then drive your knee straight into the opponent.

HEEL TACTICS

A "heel" is a contemptible person. Heel tactics are those somewhat unacceptable, painful, disruptive, and unusual techniques that won't always end a fight but will often give you the edge you need to gain the upper hand. The expression was common in the days of carnival wrestling before and just after World War II. A carnival wrestler taking on a local fighter who was giving him a difficult time would often resort to "heel tactics," including butting, biting, diving, the vee block, and pressure points. These tactics are contemptible if used on you, but they're good to know when the chips are down!

Butting

To execute a head butt, you want to hit with the area of your head that would be covered if you were wearing a hat. The part of your opponent you want to hit is the part of his head that would not be covered if he were wearing a hat. On the ground you can drive your head into him almost any time you are on top and not tied up. Standing, grab the front of his shirt and jerk him into the head butt.

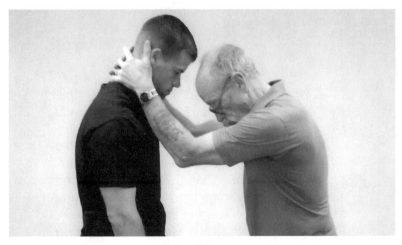

Head butt.

Also practice grabbing the back of his neck or head and jerking him into the head butt. Naturally, your opponent will not appreciate this tactic and will try to jerk his head back; you can control his head by resting your forearms on his clavicles and putting your fingers on the back of his head. This maneuver gives you leverage to tip his head forward so you can give him a second chance to appreciate your technique. As a special treat, you can alternate head butts with knees to the groin.

Biting

We were waiting for the liberty launch to take us back to the ship in Naples, Italy, when the chief hospital corpsman and a machinist mate first class suddenly hit the deck in a rolling brawl. Before we could get to them to break it up, the chief latched onto the machinist mate's cheek like a snapping turtle.

Any time your teeth are close enough to snap onto some part of your opponent's anatomy you can do lasting damage, break holds, and even end the fight.

There is always the worry of AIDS, hepatitis, and other blood-borne diseases, but if your life is at stake it is worth the risk.

Diving

Greg had exchanged words with this other guy several times in the restaurant, and I could tell he was fuming. He was standing behind me as I finished paying our bill, and the guy walked up behind us. As I turned around, the guy started to say something, but Greg lunged forward, grabbing the man's lapels with both hands and then, with a sort of leaping lunge, drove his knee into the guy's solar plexus. Guy hits deck, we hit door, everyone else hits the roof.

This is a gap-closing maneuver that almost always works well for attacking. It also works well against a punch. When you sense the punch coming, lunge into him as you drive both hands together and up toward his upper body/head.

As you lunge forward, keep your chin down and your elbows bent (straight elbows are easier to dislocate). The foot of your lead leg lifts slightly off the floor, and your rear leg stays somewhat extended behind you.

Grasp the front of his shirt with both hands and pull him into a head butt or drive a knee into his groin or abdomen. Alternatively, you can grasp the back of his head or neck and pull him into a head butt.

Another option is to stick your thumbs into his eyes, grab the back of his head or the front of his shirt, and head-butt or knee him. (No you won't blind him; despite what many "experts" may tell you, it is a lot harder to gouge out someone's eye than some would have you believe.) You can stick your thumb or finger in it and make

Dive.

it water and temporarily blind him, or even give him some short-term injury. If you want to gouge it out, you have to steady that head with the crook of your elbow (or other means) and use your thumb to do the dirty work. I do not recommend doing this because I wouldn't want to blind someone; plus it requires you to tie up both of your hands for several seconds while he has both hands free. Which means while you are gouging he can get to a concealed weapon and end your life. I have seen two eye gouge attempts, and both failed due to the same thing: the gougee was so enraged that he just went insane and beat the living daylights out of the gouger.

You can also wrap your arms around your attacker's body and effect a throw, as shown in the photo.

The Vee Block

Watch an old tape of Gene Fullmer, a former middleweight boxing champion from the fifties, and you will see a master of the vee block. He would simply wrap one

Vee block.

arm around his lower face so that it was in the vee of his elbow, and then charge in, closing the gap and then fighting on the inside. Your opponent's blows slide off the outside of your forearm, triceps, and skull. I have occasionally used this for closing the gap, but the primary purpose is for protecting your head when someone grabs your upper body.

Pressure Points

The most effective pressure points I know of are on the head. A hard blow to the chin, jaw, temple, base of skull, throat, or side/back of neck will stun or knock out an opponent. Those are the only pressure-point knockouts I have ever seen performed with the hand.

A shod kick or blunt object will score a stun or knockout blow even on the crown of the head.

Following is a list of pain points that I have used while grappling to break holds. As far as I know, none of them will be more than a painful annoyance to an opponent,

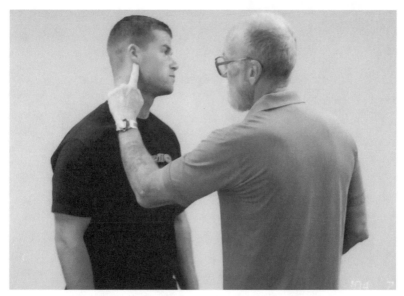

The hollow behind your ear, just at the base.

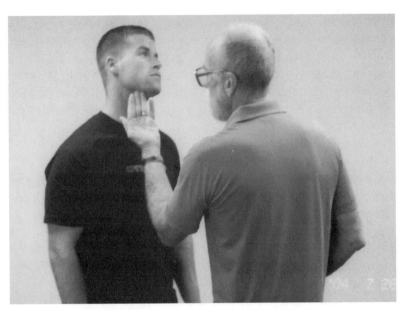

Under the jaw about midway between the chin and the angle of the jawbone.

Inside the sternal notch; push toward the armpit.

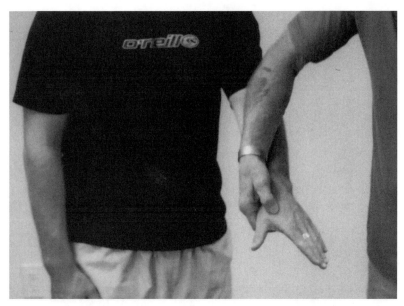

In the web of the hand, just out from where the index finger and thumb join the wrist.

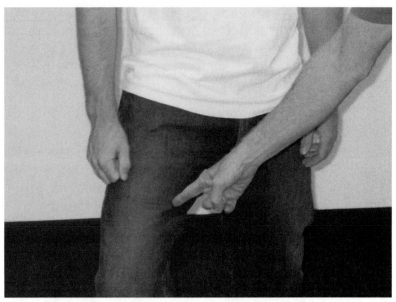

The hollow of the thigh; use the elbow or a punch for this one.

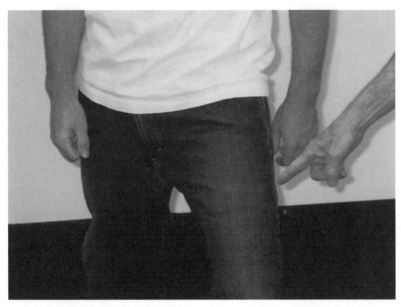

The outside of the thigh; use a punch or knee thrust here.

but they may gain you a momentary advantage that will enable you to break out of a difficult situation without injuring your attacker. Feel for the points listed and learn to use them on others; simply apply pressure with your thumb or fingertips.

THROWS

Outside the Enlisted Men's Club at the Naval Training Center, San Diego, the guy behind grabbed me around the upper arms with a bear hug as his buddy headed my way. I spread my arms slightly and twisted my body as I swung my left foot behind me and then behind his feet and continued to twist. Pushing him backward over my left leg, I kicked the heel of his left foot forward with my left instep and lifted up on his body with both arms. He was now cradled in my arms like a baby. The only thing to do when you are cradling a guy bigger than you are is to throw him on the ground, so I did.

Throws work. They work best when your opponent ends up on the ground and you are still standing. Unfortunately, that is not the way they go most of the

Cradle throw.

time. Most of the time it is a trip, and you both go to the ground, or he hangs on like a sensible brawler and takes you to the ground with him. When this happens you want to try to make yourself land on top of your opponent, hopefully with your knee in his groin, your thumb up his nose, and your free hand slamming into his neck. There's a whole chapter on ground fighting, but let's talk about a few simple throws first. These simple throws work easier and don't expose your back to your opponent as do some of the more spectacular throws you've probably seen demonstrated. Keep your face buried in his side or in your arms to protect your eyes.

Cradle Throw. I described my version of what I call the cradle throw at the start of this section. It was one of those things that happen when you are trying to do something else. I had never been taught or even read about using that throw. The fundamental part of it is the step around that puts you with one foot behind your opponent and your chest pressed snugly to his side.

You can reach this point from a rear grab as I did, from a headlock, or just by diving in and wrapping your arms around his chest as you maneuver to his side. Once you reach this point you can kick or just put your foot on his heel and throw him by twisting and pushing his body. You can also reach up his back, over his shoulder, and grab his eyes/nose/chin and pull backward as you kick or prop his heel. You can also simply reach up with your free hand that is not wrapped around his waist and push on his face to break his balance and dump him. At any time in this setup, you can slam in a few shots to the family jewels using your fist or the thumb side of your forearm. If you feel particularly nasty, take that ballpoint pen out of your shirt pocket and slam the sharp end of it into his family jewels. He will probably decide to do some sprinting of his own.

Tripping Throw. This is a schoolboy throw that almost

Tripping throw.

always works well. Close the gap, dive in, wrap your arms around his chest, and then wrap one of your legs around one of his like a grapevine and pull it toward you as you push him backward in the direction of the disabled leg. You can wrap from either the inside or the outside of his leg. This throw works best when you are still facing your opponent rather than after you've moved to his side, but I have used it when I was at the person's side, too. Practice it from the front, from the side, and using both the inner and outer leg wrap.

FOOTWORK

Frankly, footwork is vital. Practice at least the following:

- In your fighting stance, shuffle your feet as you move about, moving your lead foot a few inches and then following with your rear foot, moving your left foot to your left and then following with your right. Continue by moving the foot that is in the direction you want to go first and then following with the other foot. Go in every direction and add turns as well. Never cross your feet.
- Practice sweeping your right hand toward the center of your body and swinging your left leg in an arc as you twist to get out of the way of an onrushing opponent. Then practice in the other direction.
- Practice the step-around used in the cradle throw.
- Sprint. From any position you can think of, suddenly sprint in any direction for a few steps. If you can do it, the best maneuver of all is to get the heck out of the area.
- Jump rope at least 10 minutes a day if possible. This is a great footwork builder.
- Occasionally practice all of your standing techniques in extremely slow motion; this helps develop balance and coordination.

Breakaways

ully half of all attacks start out with a grab of some kind. The attacker simply wants to control you until he can get you in a position that allows him to do damage without endangering himself. The instant you see the grab coming or are grabbed, go into action. (You do not have to complete the combinations given here if the person grabbing you turns out to be a friend who is just goofing around.) When you practice, do the whole combination, and if you practice on some sort of training dummy, do it full force. (This is why I recommend using the most lifelike training apparatus you can find.)

Most of the breakaways presented in this chapter end with either a cradle or tripping throw or with the suggestion to sprint, dive, or strike. If you can end the confrontation by sprinting away, that is always the safest option; if you cannot, you must continue the confrontation until you can either get away or disable the attacker. Diving in to effect a throw is always a good option because it gets you out of your opponent's striking range, but it also puts you in a position where you may have to go to the ground with him. Striking (with hands or feet) may disable/disorient him and give you the opportunity to sprint, but again, it leaves you in his striking zone. Keep in mind that if he is behind you, stomping down along his shin and into his instep is a good move; if he lifts you off the ground, kick backward into his legs and groin with your heels. Snapping your head back into his face may also give you the opening you need to escape. There is no sure way of ending a violent confrontation without getting hurt.

WRIST GRABS

A grab that quickly escalates into a confrontation is the wrist grab. I have mostly seen this happen when people are having a verbal confrontation and one tries to end it by turning or walking away. The person who wants to continue will grab the other person's wrist and hold it to keep him from leaving. Things usually go downhill from there.

- *From the front.* Anytime someone grabs your wrist or arm, pull and rotate your wrist so that you are pulling against the opening between his thumb and fingers, using the strength of your upper arm. At the same time, deliver the PHT to the nose with your free hand. This will almost always result in breaking the grab and put you in position to deliver a straight punch to the throat. Sprint, dive, or strike. Practice this several times as though someone was grabbing your wrist with one or both hands and as if someone was grabbing your elbow.
- *From the side.* Do the same thing, rotating and pulling to free yourself from the attacker. You are not normally in the right position to deliver the PHT, so get both hands up in front of you so you can either sprint, dive, or strike.
- *From the rear.* Do the same thing, rotating and pulling to free yourself from the attacker. Sprint, dive, or strike.

Wrist grab pull-out.

LAPEL GRABS

I didn't even know where the guy came from or what his problem was. He just walked up to me in a restaurant in San Diego, grabbed the front of my shirt with his left hand, and started to yell something. I slammed his elbow with my right palm and, as he spun to his right, lunged forward in the dive, pushing him with both hands so he stumbled into an unoccupied table. Several of his friends grabbed him and hustled him out the door, explaining that he'd had too much to drink. A good way for things to end; no one got hurt. Had I stood there listening to what he had to say, I might have ended up eating a fist.

When someone grabs your lapel(s) or the front of your shirt, it is not because he has good intentions. Any of sev-

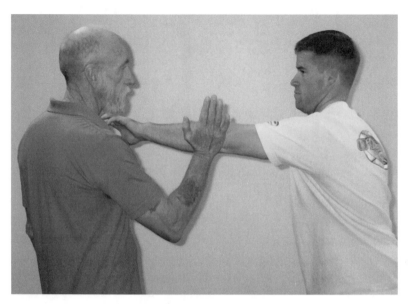

Palm heel to elbow.

eral things are about to happen: (1) He will jerk you into a head butt. (2) He will hold you with one hand and feed you much fist with the other. (3) He will pull your lapels down over your shoulders and then, while your arms are somewhat immobilized by your jacket, knock knots on your face faster than you can count them. I have seen every one of these grabbing attacks used successfully; fortunately, it was not on me.

Anytime someone reaches for you, use the PHT to his arm(s) to knock his hands upward or toward his centerline. That is simply the direction in which you are stronger and the other guy is weaker. If his hand happens to be tangled in your clothing, his elbow may be dislocated. It doesn't take too much pressure to cause a dislocation. Sprint, dive, or strike.

If someone actually grabs you, reach over his hand(s) to grab the back of one of his hands, placing your elbow in the vee-block position because his next maneuver will

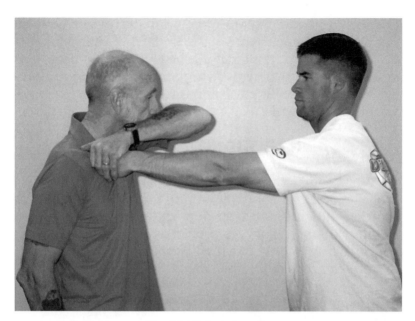

Vee-block lapel grab.

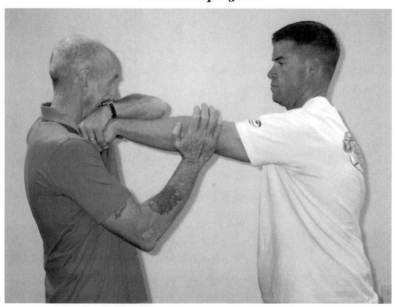

Vee block and palm heel to elbow.

probably be to punch or head-butt you. Now that you have stabilized his hand, slam your palm heel into his elbow. If his arm is more or less straight, the elbow will probably be dislocated. If his elbow is bent, you will be lifting it, forcing him to release his grasp and turn somewhat to the side. Sprint, dive, or strike.

REAR SHOULDER GRABS

When someone grabs your shoulder from the rear, he is probably going to spin you around for a confrontation or a sucker punch. Place your opposite hand on top of his, forming the vee block to protect your head, and swing your free arm in an arc that will strike his elbow (hopefully from the outside). Either way, it will break his grip on your shoulder and give you the opportunity to sprint, dive, or strike.

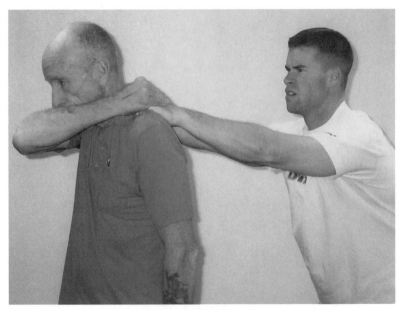

Rear grab; form the vee block.

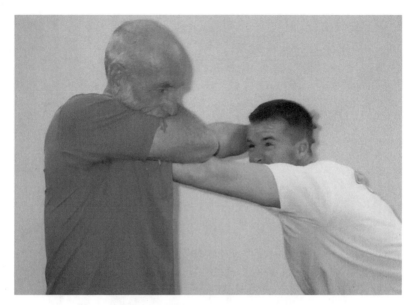

Swinging your arm over his elbow.

FULL NELSON

The full nelson is generally used by someone who wants to immobilize you for a short period of time while he rests or while his friends punch your face in (or both). You are in a full nelson when someone behind you has reached under your arms so that his inner elbows are in your armpits and his hands are clasped behind your neck.

Clasp your hands together, place them on your forehead, and, using the strength of your neck and arms, push your head backward. This loosens his hold somewhat, and you can often jerk your elbows straight down and break the hold. Sprint or spin inside his arms and dive in for the throw.

If he has a powerful grip and interlocks his fingers to hold you in the full nelson, you may not be able to break the hold. In that case, grab one of his fingers and pull it back toward his wrist to either break the hold or dislocate his finger.

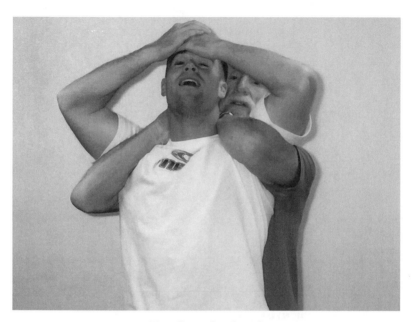

Hands to forehead.

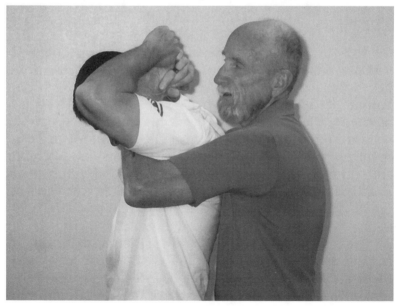

Finger grab.

38 STRICTLY STREET STUFF

HEADLOCK

You don't want to stay in a headlock very long because you are either going to get punched, rammed into something solid, or thrown to the ground. None of these are very inviting.

He may start striking you while keeping your head secured in the crook of his elbow, so reach around his back and grab the upper arm of his striking hand just above the elbow. This will either stop or reduce the effectiveness of his strikes. Now fire off a few of your own right into his groin, or place your thumb just inside the bony protuberance of the inner part of his elbow and push his arm far enough out that you are able to slip your head out of the hold. Sprint, dive, or strike. (Yes, the dive works well from the rear as well.)

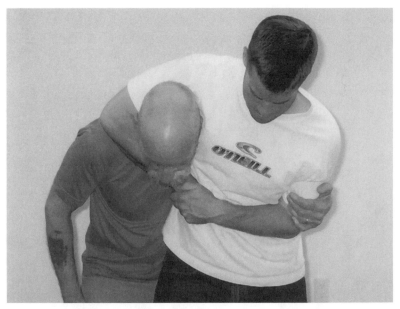

Reach around his back and grab his biceps.

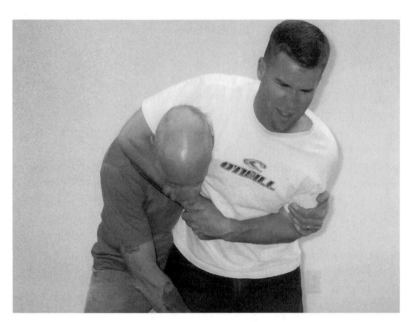

Strike his groin.

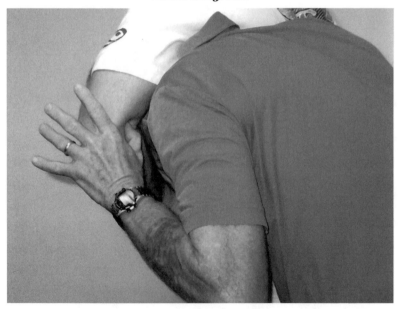

Push your thumb into his inner elbow.

FRONT TWO-HAND CHOKE

He tries to choke you by grabbing your neck with both hands and squeezing. Strike both his elbows with your palm heels, driving them up and away from your neck. Immediately follow with a knee to the groin.

Another alternative is to reach back and grab one of his fingers with one hand while you stabilize his wrist with your other hand, dislocate his finger, and then follow with a vertical fist punch to the face and a straight punch to the throat.

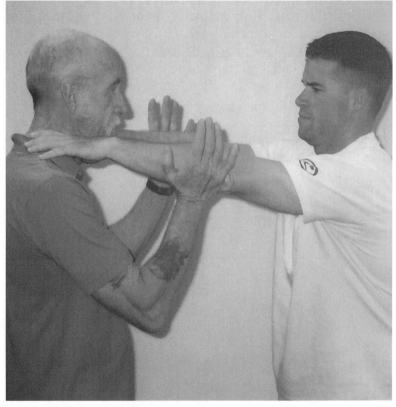

Strike his elbows.

REAR NAKED CHOKE

I have ended quite a few fights by using the rear naked choke but don't recommend using this for street survival for the reasons mentioned in the introduction. Get out of this hold quickly and viciously; you only have seconds before unconsciousness sets in.

As you see/feel those arms going around your neck, drive both hands upward in a double PHT, and knock the arms up over your head as you duck down. Then either sprint away or spin and dive in for the throw.

Another option is to pull out that ballpoint pen and stab it into the underside of your attacker's arm near the elbow, forcing the arm up over your head. Then sprint, or spin and dive in for the throw.

If you don't have a pen or knife, you must turn your chin into the crook of his arm to relieve pressure on your throat, pull down on his elbow to relieve more of the pres-

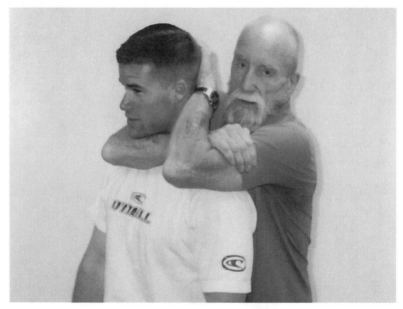

The rear naked choke.

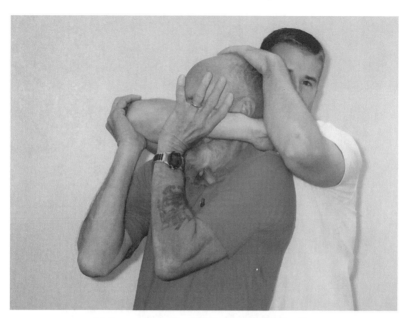

Drive upward with your palm heels.

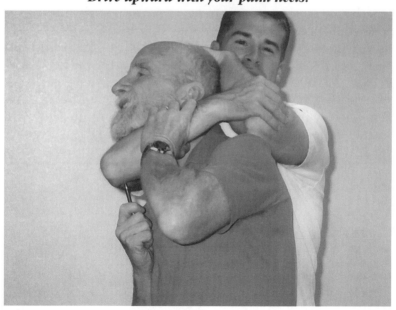

Stab him with a ballpoint.

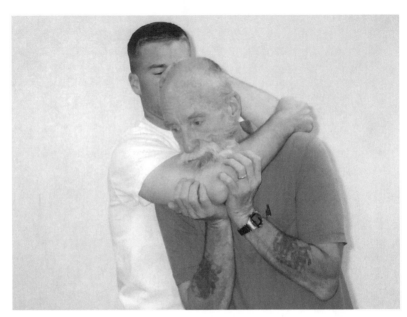

Turn into the vee.

sure, and then reach up over your shoulder and either grab and dislocate a finger or rake his eyes as you stomp his foot. At any small release of pressure, push his arm up and get out of this hold.

Another possibility is to squat slightly, hold on to his arm with both hands, and then throw him right over your head. An experienced street fighter will hold on to your neck when you throw him and take you right over with him, possibly breaking your neck. I don't recommend trying this throw.

BEAR HUG

This may sound like a nothing deal, but it is not. You are about to be thrown on your head, and it will probably knock you out. Get out of this hold as soon as possible.

- *Over your arms from the front.* Place the heels of your

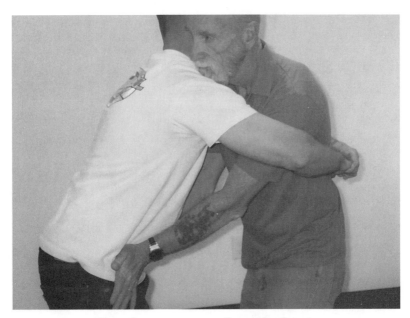

Bear hug over arms from the front.

hands against his hips and brace your upper arms against your sides. Push his hips away from yours, slam your knee into his groin, and head-butt his face. As soon as his grip relaxes, either dive in for the throw or spin and sprint.

- *Over your arms from the rear.* Suddenly squat slightly as you push your arms out from your sides. You will gain a few inches of maneuvering room so you can turn inside his arms and then apply the cradle throw.
- *Under your arms from the front.* Place your thumbs in his eyes and push. He either releases you or loses his sight. Spin and sprint, knee and head-butt, or dive in for the throw.
- *Under your arms from the rear.* Pull that pen out of your shirt pocket and stick it into his hands to loosen his hold. Or push down against his hands with your thumbs and stomp his foot to loosen it. Then sprint away, or spin and go for the throw.

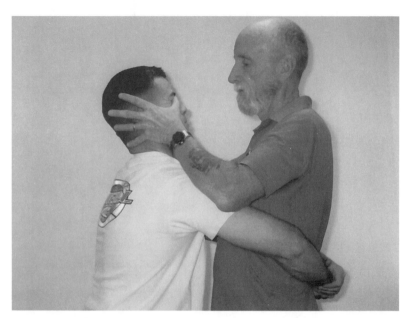

Bear hug under arms from the front.

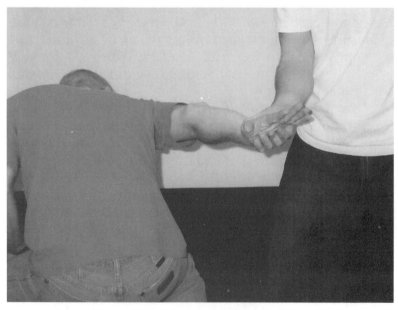

Squat down and spin to the side.

HAMMER LOCK

Once this thing is fully locked in, it is almost impossible to get out of. As soon as the attempt is made, squat down and spin to the side as you straighten your arm. Now it is a side wrist grab, so pull your arm away from his grasp and dive in for the throw or sprint away.

Defending against Various Blows and Throws

his chapter deals with the most important problem in most fights that do not involve weapons: the fact that someone is trying to knock or throw you to the ground. Merely hitting the ground from a throw will sometimes stun you. A punch or kick that puts you down definitely does. Once you are on the ground you lose much of your mobility, and without the strength of your legs and waist, your punches are not as powerful. To add insult to injury, your opponent's friends are much more likely to jump in and put the boots to you. Try to avoid the ground unless it gives you a definite advantage, such as friends with boots.

TAKEDOWNS

Takedowns can include any kind of throw or trip and are meant to give the initiating party an advantage when both of you hit the ground. If you are going down, grab on and take your opponent with you. Try to twist so you wind up on top, and try to attack his vital spots: joints, genitals, neck, and eyes. You'll see a lot more on this in the chapter on ground grappling.

An attacker initiating a takedown will try to lunge in low to grab you around the hips, thighs, or even one leg, and then drive you into the ground with the power of the lunge. The following are some effective defenses against takedowns.

Snap-Down and Kick

Push your attacker down and to the side with a double-handed palm strike to the head and/or shoulders. Follow up by sprinting away, kicking him, or looking for a weapon to use while he is on the ground and you are erect.

Snap-down.

Sprawl

Sometimes your opponent is too fast, and you cannot do a snap-down. Grab his upper body and kick your legs out straight behind you, preventing him from effecting the takedown by falling on top of him. This should place him face down on the deck and you on top with your head roughly between his shoulder blades. Hold on and start slamming those knees into his head if he is still conscious after having endured a forced face plant.

Tip of the Balance

When you are grappling erect with someone who is trying to throw you, try to throw off his balance by tipping

Sprawl.

his head away from you as you pull his waist or legs toward you. As a last resort, go with the throw and take him with you to the ground.

KICKS

Defending against kicks is a matter of avoiding, catching, deflecting, or blocking. Avoiding mostly just involves footwork and body twists. Catching, while difficult, gives you a real advantage. Deflecting and blocking are so similar that their difference is mostly just in application. Block as a last resort, because you have to absorb the power of the kick to block it.

The following are some effective defenses against kicks.

Scoop Block and Shove
I learned this technique in the middle of a fight.

Scoop block.

The guy fired a high front kick to my groin when my hands were low. I just sort of automatically twisted slightly to the side and scooped his kick, so I wound up holding his ankle by the crook of my elbow.

Once you've scooped his kick, simply diving forward into the opponent will put him on the ground (he has already lost his balance because you are holding one of his legs up off of the ground). Alternatively, you can fire off a kick of your own at this point—after all, there are uncomfortable areas highly exposed.

Shin Block and Punches

Thai boxers are masters of this maneuver and have to be because they are squared off against some awesome kickers. When you see the kick coming, simply raise one

Shin block.

knee so that you are able to catch the kick with your knee or shin. The Thais seem to mainly use this against the roundhouse kick, but it will work against front and side kicks as well. Using this block generally seems to put the defender in the position to follow the block with a jab/straight punch combination leading with the side that used the knee block.

Elbow Clamp and Forearm Blow

This is another technique I just sort of happened upon. It works well.

I was sparring with a high-ranking karateka when he fired off a rib-high roundhouse kick. Instead of taking it on my forearm and upper arm as I usually did, I simply raised my elbow and then clamped it down on his kicking leg,

Elbow clamp.

trapping it between my ribs and upper arm. He dropped his guard, trying to regain his balance, and I whacked his chest with my other forearm to break his balance. It is really hard to stand up when someone is holding your leg more than waist high and hitting you at the same time, so he dropped to the floor, and I stepped away.

PUNCHES

The dive and the vee block were covered in the chapter on mechanics because they are so useful in all forms of self-protection. They are especially good for defending against punches. The following are some other possibilities.

Slip
The slip involves slightly shifting your head and body

Slipping a punch.

weight to the side while simultaneously bending your knees. It is usually the best means of avoiding the full power of a straight punch. If you slip enough to cause a full miss, that is great, but simply slipping enough to keep you from taking the full power of the punch can mean the difference between surviving and losing. Practice by hanging up a small bag or padded stick and swinging it away from you. When it comes back toward your face, "slip" the punch.

Bob

Drop your weight by bending your knees, and cant your head a bit further forward, lowering it as well. If the punch misses completely, this is wonderful. If it hits the top of your head it won't do much damage to your fighting ability, but it may break your opponent's knuckles because the crown of your head is rock-hard. (I'm sure your wife or mother has already told you how hard-headed you are.)

Bobbing.

Chapter 4

Preemptive Attacks

ou have no doubt heard that a good offense is the best defense. When you know that you are going to have to fight for your life, don't wait until the opponent decides to initiate. He is trying to put himself in a win-win situation. You can start it when he is not expecting it and put him in a lose-lose situation.

I walked into a small bar in Hong Kong to have a beer while wearing my cute little white sailor suit. I ordered, and as the barkeep brought it to me a British Marine walked up and said, "You can't drink in here; this is a Marine bar. My eyes had adjusted to the gloom, and I realized that, aside from the bartender and me, there were only British Marines and bar girls in the place. Trying to be nice and save face as well, I said, "OK, I'll just finish my beer and leave." The Marine was twice my size, and his buddies were beginning to gather around him as he said, "No, you can just get the *#@%

out now." I backed the 10 feet or so to the open door and onto the sidewalk outside. As this huge Marine came through the door with all his buddies trapped behind him, I fired off my best front kick ever. I could literally feel his male anatomy through the leather of my shoe. Then I fled through the streets of Hong Kong with at least a full squad of British Marines in hot pursuit. They were fueled with anger; I was fueled with pure terror. Fortunately, terror won that race. Sprinting is always a good option.

- *Front kick to groin.* Practice this puppy as you walk up to the victim and as you stand in front of him. You want it to be a total surprise. Practice in front of a mirror and try to make sure you do not telegraph your intentions by looking at his groin, raising your hands unnaturally, or any such other movements.
- *Dive in, grab, knee, and/or head-butt.* This was pretty well covered in the previous chapter. Use it at close range for attacking.
- *Palm heel thrust.* You already learned the PHT in the mechanics chapter and used it as part of some breakaways. This is another one to use at close range to initiate the attack. Practice it in front of a mirror to avoid telegraphing and on an apparatus that can simulate a chin to fire the PHT into.
- *Front kick and/or dive.* Fire off that front kick to the lower legs for a distraction and follow it with a dive. Sometimes you can just forget the distraction and dive right in. Practice all of the possible follow-throughs to a dive—tripping throws, head butt, knee, cradle throw, groin punches, biting, and foot stomping.

Ground Grappling

I t was a bar fight in Memphis, Tennessee, and the whole place was going nuts. I only knew one guy, and he was already on the floor unconscious. It seemed like everyone there was fighting each other, throwing things, and trying to get out the door at the same time. Some fat guy shot in, did a double-leg pickup on me, and just about drove me through the floor. I had him in my guard, but all I could do was cover up as he delivered a sharp rain of punches to my head. I actually heard someone say, "Let me take his glasses off before you break them in his eyes." Then a pitcher of beer hit him in the back of the head. I loved it.

In probably half of the physical confrontations you get into, you will wind up rolling around on the ground with your opponent. This is not where you want to be! You want to be on your feet and moving, and you want him to be on the ground and moving very slowly or not at all.

With ground fighting, in addition to the problem of bystanders, there is the problem of being at such close range that you cannot see everything your opponent is doing. With most of the submission-type holds, the person applying the hold is using both hands, while the one being choked out or forced into submission has one or both hands free. The savvy street fighter will use that free hand to obtain a weapon and use it. If you go to the ground with someone, use any weapon you can grab to increase the force of your strikes—a rock or knife will do tremendous damage and is hard to defend against. Don't hold someone unless you are a law enforcement official or someone else who has backup in the melee. When you grab someone, keep moving; don't lie there and expect him to submit. If you grab his finger to break a hold, finish up by dislocating the finger and moving on toward your goal of getting back on your feet.

This chapter is not necessarily organized according to a progression of events that is going to happen in a ground fight. This particular sequence is used because it is an easy way to practice the flow of movements. Again, feel free to modify this so it complements your training and experience.

YOU ARE IN HIS GUARD

A person has you in his guard when he is on his back and you are between his legs. In the closed guard he will wrap his legs around you and lock his ankles to hold you in place while he secures a choke or arm lock. He can strike from this position, but not with full power. He can also strike with his heels by holding you with one leg and using the other to drive his heel into your kidney area. You do not want to stay there and grapple. Keep moving, hurt him, and get on your feet.

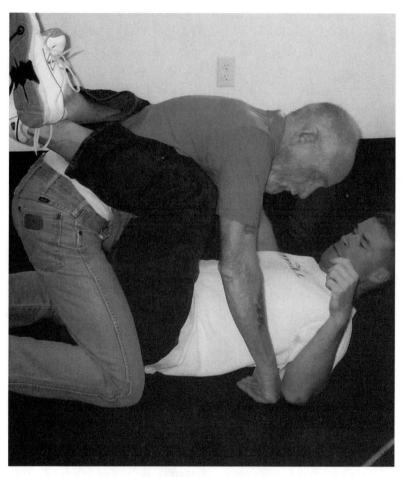

The guard position.

- Hold one or both of his hands or arms and repeatedly butt him in the face.

Head butt in the guard.

- Deliver a rain of punches to his face and neck. It seems best to strike with a vertical fist or palm heel to the face and then a straight punch to the throat.

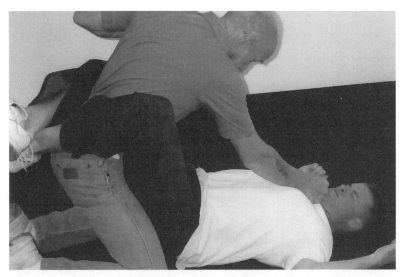

Straight punches in the guard.

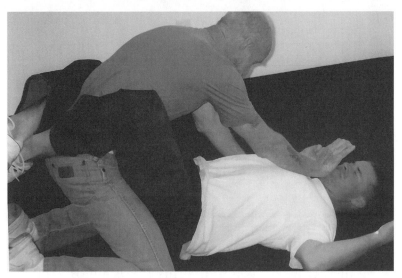

PHT in the guard.

• When he reaches for you, you can often grab his wrist and then use the elbow of your same hand to strike his face repeatedly.

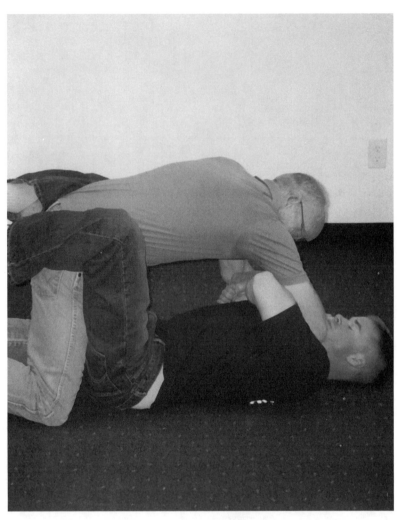

Elbow strikes in the guard.

- If he reaches for you so that his arm is almost straight, stabilize his wrist and then strike his elbow with your palm heel or elbow to dislocate it.

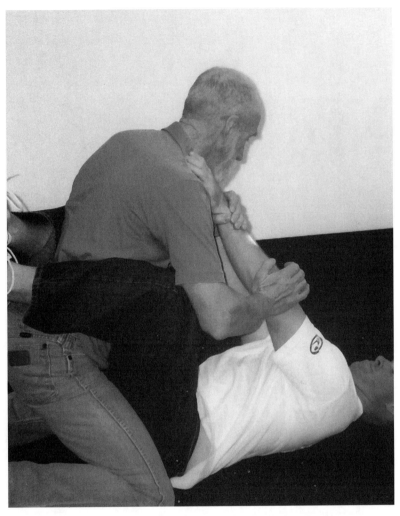

Stabilize his wrist and strike his elbow in the guard.

- If he grabs behind your head to pull you down, you can reach back and dislocate one of his fingers and then continue pounding away.

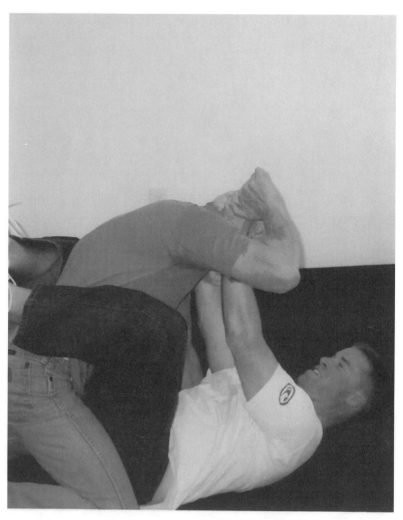

Finger grab to break away in guard.

- Often when he tries to grab your head, you can drive your elbow back between your body and his arm to free yourself from the grab and then push his arm down across his face and resume pounding him.

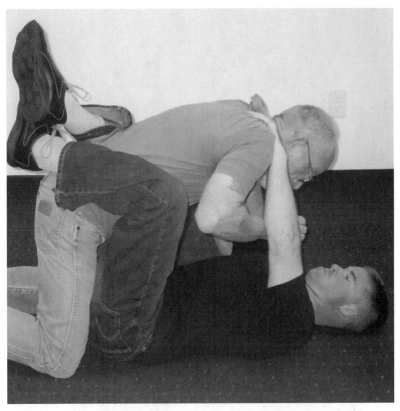

Using your elbow to break his head grab.

- If you are pulled into him, start biting anywhere you can and rubbing your fingers into his eyes or stuffing one or both thumbs up his nostrils. As soon as you regain access, resume pounding away.
- Sometimes you can sit up, raise one leg so that that foot is flat on the floor and he is sort of half twisted. Then force your elbow between his thigh and your body. When you can get your whole arm through, reach around and grab the front of his shirt as his leg hold around your body separates. At this point you can start kneeing and striking him from the side and finally straddle him. You have just achieved the mount.

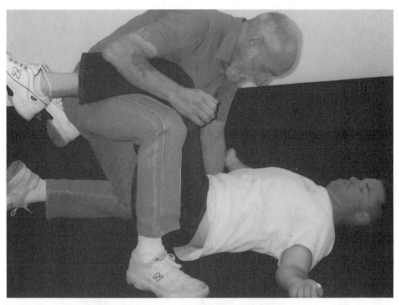

Raise your leg to start breakaway.

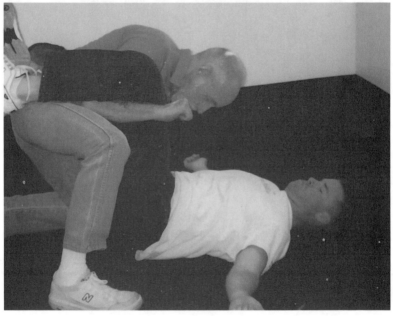

Elbow between his thigh and your body.

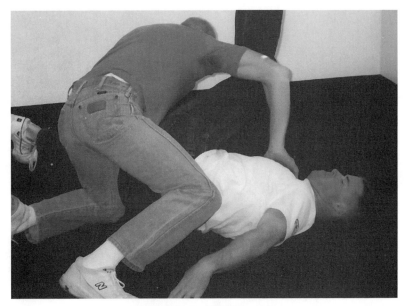

Force the hold to break.

YOU HAVE MOUNTED

When you have achieved the mount you are in a great position to pound away. At this point you can do all the pounding that was listed in the previous section. In addition, you can grab his head pull it toward you and then slam it into the ground repeatedly. He will try to get you off by

- *Pushing at one of your knees so he can work his leg free.* Pull up on his elbows to negate that push and then resume pounding.
- *Locking one of your legs and getting both of his feet flat on the floor so he can quickly shove his hips upward (boompsadaisy) and then to the side so he rolls you off to the side where he can regain control.* Drive the leg he is trying to lock down to break his attempt and keep pounding away.

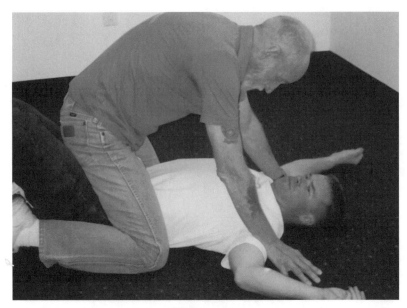

The mount.

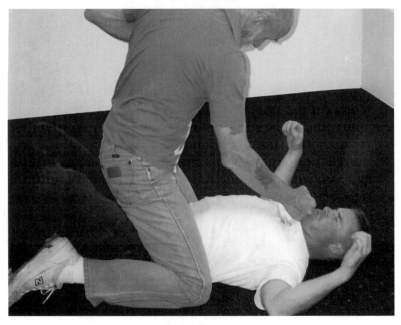

Pound away.

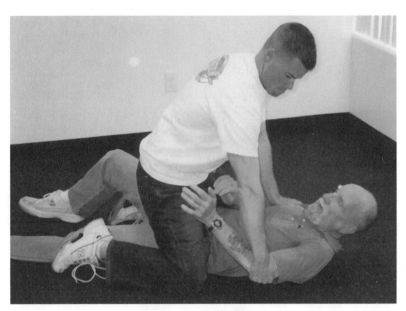

Pull up on his elbow.

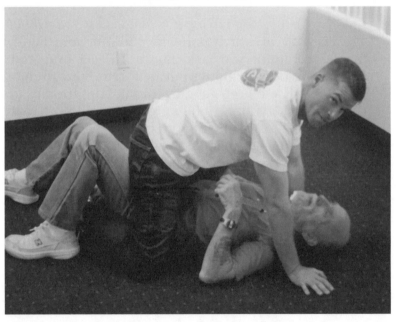

Locking your leg before trying to throw you out of the mount.

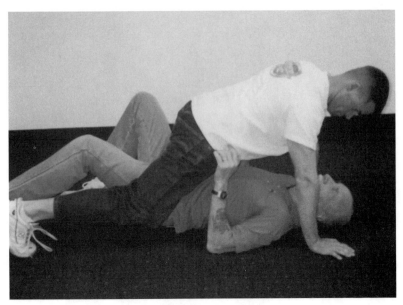

Driving past his lock.

- *Grabbing your belt and trying to boompsadaisy you right up over his head,* at which point he will bite your family jewels, prompting you to do anything to get away from this nut. When he grabs your belt, ram both thumbs into his eyes and keep gouging, or put both thumbs up his nose and try to bury them to the wrist. More than likely he will turn loose of your belt.
- *Grabbing you and pulling you down to him.* Use the escapes listed in the section titled, "You Are in His Guard."
- *Trying to roll over to get away from your pounding.* Allow him to roll, but keep yourself stabilized. When he has his back to you, start slamming the base of his skull with your palm heel or elbows. If you get tired of this, start pulling his head toward you and then slamming his face into the ground.

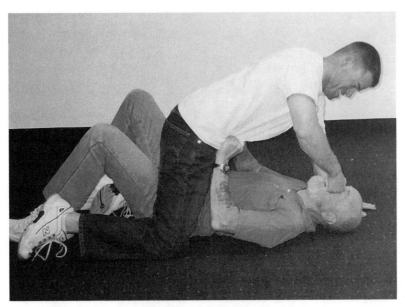

Thumbing his eyes.

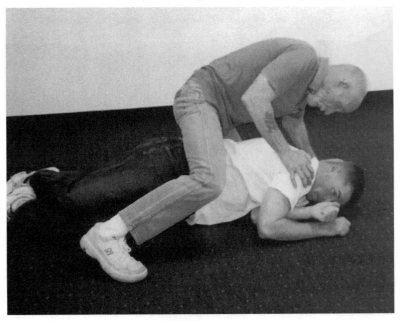

Let him roll.

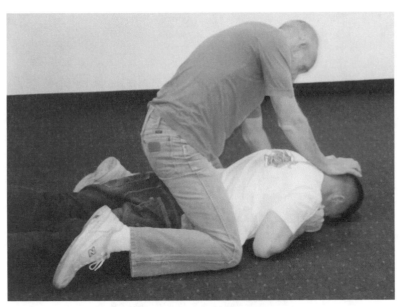

Palm heel the back of his head.

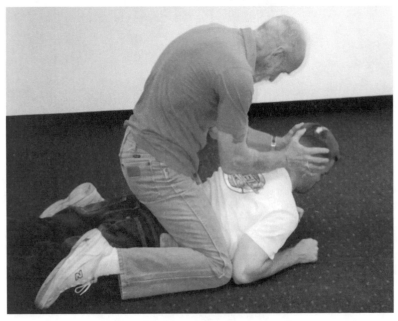

Slam his face into the ground.

YOU ARE IN HIS MOUNT

You are in deep trouble. Try all the escapes we just went over in the last section. Push his knee with your elbow and then your hand(s), and slide one leg free and then work the other until you have achieved the guard position. Lock one of his ankles and then boompsadaisy upward and twist to throw him off to one side. Grab his belt, boompsadaisy him straight over your head, and bite him in painful places. Get your hands on his butt and push him on past your head. Grab the back of his head and pull him down as you push up on his chin with the other hand, forcing him to roll off or get an injured neck. Pull him straight down and stick your thumb into his eye or nose, or grab his throat and crush it with one hand as you stabilize his head with the other.

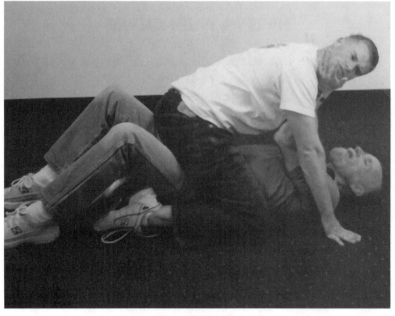

Head twist.

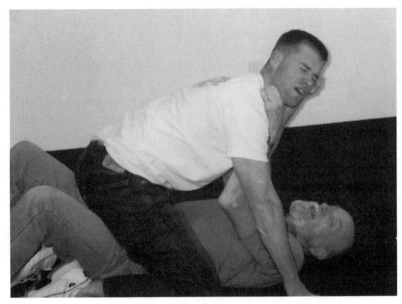

Throat crush.

HE IS IN YOUR GUARD

This is not a jujitsu match, and you do not want to lie here in your guard until you can work yourself into a position to secure a choke or arm lock.

- If you can, pull him down and stabilize his head while you do the eye-raking, nose-thumbing, throat-grabbing thing.
- If he stands, grab his ankles and hold them, then push with your butt to make him fall backward; as he does, roll up and try to achieve the mount.
- Stabilize his arms as best as you can with your hands, bend one knee and put that foot flat on the ground, push that foot downward so you slide far enough to put your other foot on his hip or abdomen, and then push him away with the foot that is on his hip as you draw the other one up and kick him in the face with it. Get out from under him and get up.

Grab his ankles and push.

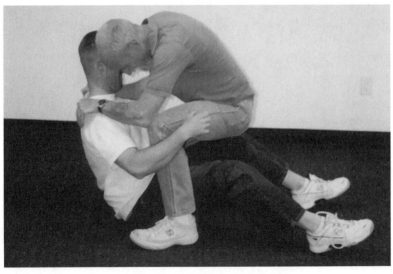

Roll up into mount.

GROUND GRAPPLING **77**

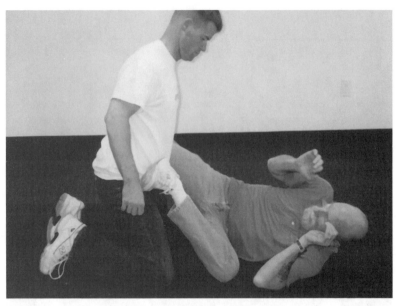

Foot-on-abdomen push-away.

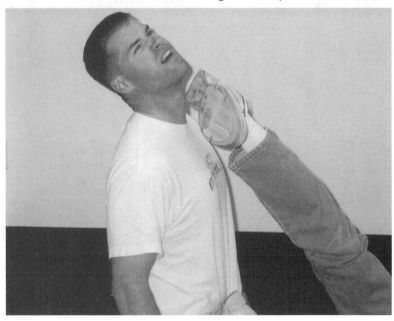

Kick his face.

HE IS STANDING, AND YOU ARE DOWN

If your opponent is standing and you are on the ground, try to spin on your back so your feet are always toward him and kick with your heels any time he is within range. This is desperation time; seize any moment you can to get back on your feet.

HE HAS YOU IN A REAR SCISSORS HOLD

If he manages to get you in a scissors hold from the rear (his legs are around you and his ankles are locked), lock your ankles around his (if his right ankle is on top, put your left ankle over his and your right over yours), and then pull his toward you. This is extremely painful, and he will almost always release the lock and try to get away. This is also a good time to pull that ballpoint pen out of your pocket and stab away.

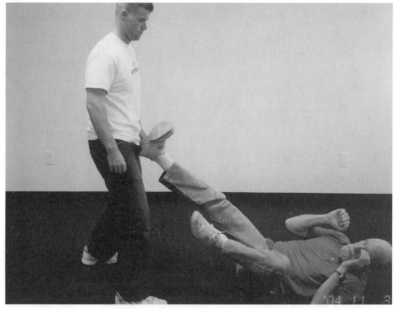

Kicking a standing opponent.

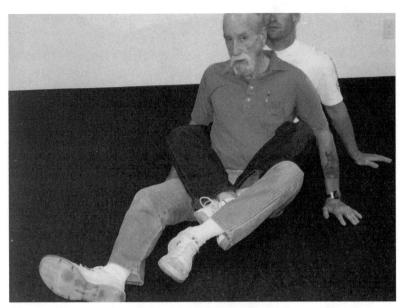

Rear scissor step 1.

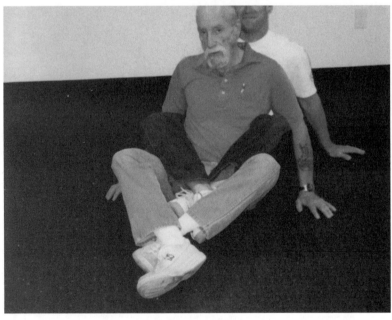

Rear scissor step 2.

HE HAS YOU IN A HEADLOCK

- If you are on the ground, on your side, with him holding you in a headlock from on top, shove the arm closest to his head between you and along his neck. When your forearm is on the side of his neck, grasp your wrist with your opposite hand and push, forcing your forearm into the side of his neck. This is extremely painful and will cause him to release you. Keep pushing until his head is near your legs and then hammer his face with your heel.
- If you are on the ground, on your side, on top of him and he has you in a headlock, then straddle him with your legs and get in a stable position before you break the headlock by pushing against his neck as you did in the breakaway above. This time when he releases his hold, you are in the mount position and can punch away.

Stabilize your position in the headlock.

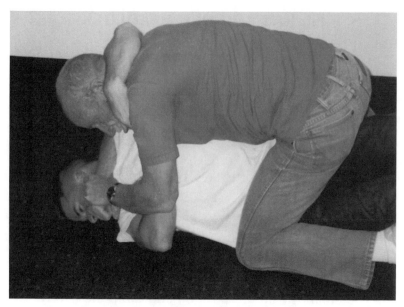

Use your forearm to effect the release.

GET UP!

You are going to be in some awkward positions on the ground, so when you are training, assume all kinds of positions on the ground and get up and moving as fast as you can. Sometimes you can roll to your feet, other times you can get one knee up and take off like a sprinter. Try every position you can think of, and practice it.

Chapter 6

Weapons

I do not recommend carrying a weapon or using one unless you are outnumbered, at a major disadvantage, or attacked with a weapon. Sometimes it is possible to anticipate things, and if you are able to anticipate a confrontation and have any choice, you should avoid the situation so there won't be any need for the weapon. If, on the other hand, you have no choice in the matter, you will probably choose to carry a weapon. Note that even when you are unarmed you still have the choice of using or not using a weapon, simply because everything around you, even the floor you are standing on, can be used as a weapon. Choosing to use something other than your hands just adds to your difficulty in dealing with the legal problems caused by close-quarter combat. The bottom line is, the consequences are too great to take this thing lightly. If you decide to use a weapon, don't threaten; just attack, get it over with, and get out of Dodge.

HANDGUNS

Pop always carried a pistol
(usually a Colt 1911 .45 ACP)

and drove really fast cars. I think it was a holdover from his days as a bootlegger during prohibition. We were on a lonely road in south Alabama late at night, headed to visit my grandma in Florida, when he stopped in the middle of the empty road. Up ahead were two cars parked, blocking the road in such a way as to allow a car to go through them, but only at about five miles per hour. Pop's orders were curt: "Everybody on the floorboards, now! This is a hijacking!" Of course, Mom and my older brother hit the deck, while I stayed right behind Pop with my head just above the seat. I wasn't about to miss any of the action. Pop idled the car along toward the parked cars, and just as we got to the first one several guys popped up out of the ditch beside the road and sprinted toward the car. Then the real show started. Pop hung that .45 out of the window with his left hand and put the pedal to the metal. As the tires screeched and the .45 boomed, the would-be hijackers were diving back into the ditch. As we went by the second car, Pop gave it a couple of rounds in the side just for the fun of it, and we were down the road like a rocket. That '41 Ford with a 3/4 race Mercury engine was pegging the needle in seconds, and the only thing those folks got from us was a look at disappearing taillights and a chance to change their shorts.

I have carried handguns in the navy and as authorized by my civilian employer, and I have also carried them a few times when it wasn't legal but I felt that my life could be in danger. There is rightly a lot of controversy about handguns, and I am not going to try to tell you what the answer should be. I will say, though, that if you decide to carry a handgun you should be firmly in control of yourself, be thoroughly trained, and have the will to use your gun if need be. Otherwise you are likely to shoot someone you don't intend to shoot or have your gun taken away and used on you. Even worse would be for an innocent child to pick up an unlocked, unsecured handgun and kill or injure himself or a playmate.

This isn't a book about gunfighting, but here are a few pointers anyway:

- Adopt a firm stance, much like a boxer's, but keep both heels on the ground.
- Hold the pistol in both hands, keeping your arms extended, and swing it up right in front of your face.
- The pistol should appear almost like a black bar sitting on top of your hands, with the front sight on your opponent at about belt-buckle level. Squeeze the trigger twice.
- Reacquire the sight picture and move to the next target.
- If you have time, and especially if the opponent is more than about 10 feet away (most gunfights occur at a range of 21 feet or less), acquire a total sight picture, lining up the front and rear sights before you squeeze the trigger.
- Practice firing with both hands from a variety of positions, and practice reloading the weapon. Practice firing after an uphill sprint when your breath is coming in ragged gasps. To simulate shooting in the rain, use a plastic training gun and get in the shower fully clothed, turn the water on cold only, and practice acquiring a sight picture. Practice taking it out of your carrying place (e.g., holster, pocket, waistband) while rolling on the ground, walking, running, and so on.

HE HAS A GUN (OH, NO!)

You are in deep trouble. If you are in any position to run or get away, do it. Make your first move away from the centerline of his body. It is easier to track a target toward the centerline than toward the outside, and so he has a better chance of hitting you if you go toward his centerline. Run and get anything you can between you and the shooter. Keep on trucking; the farther away from him, the better off you are. Even highly trained shooters have difficulty hitting a moving target with a rifle and even more difficulty with a handgun. Speed and distance are your friends.

If you are up close and he is holding a gun on you, there is some chance of getting away, but the odds are worse. On the other hand, if you feel that he is going to shoot you anyway, you might as well try. Once you launch your attack, do not stop until he is no longer a threat (i.e., running for his life or unable to continue the assault). Practice the disarms that follow with a partner if possible, always using a fake gun (never a real one), and saw off the trigger guard because most of these disarms will break the assailant's trigger finger.

Gun Held to Your Head

Snap your hand backward to strike the gun with the back of your wrist. Spin, grabbing the gun, then get both

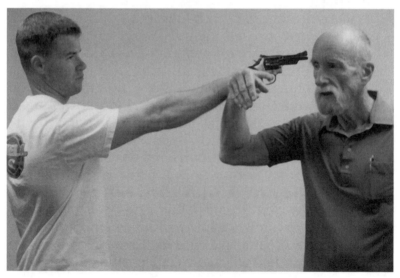

Snap your hand backward.

Tip the barrel up.

hands on the weapon, tipping the barrel straight up and then jerking it straight down, ripping it out of his hand.

If for some reason you cannot rip the gun out of his hands, keep the barrel tipped up and away from you and start pumping those knees into his groin and lower abdomen. If you are close enough, start head-butting and biting as well.

Gun Held to Your Abdomen

Twist your body to the side, out of the line of fire, as you grab the gun with whichever hand will force it toward his centerline. Again, hold on to the gun, then get both hands on it, tip the barrel straight up, and jerk it straight down, ripping it out of his hands. If for some reason you cannot rip the gun out of his hands, keep the barrel tipped up and away from you and start pumping those knees into his groin and lower abdomen. If you are close enough, start head-butting and biting too.

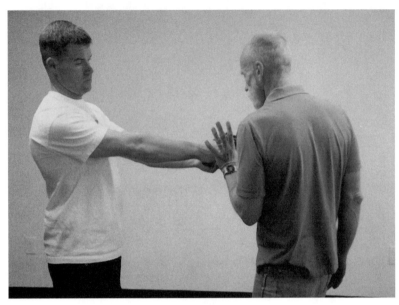

Twist and grab the gun.

Gun Held to Your Back

Twist your body to the side, out of the line of fire, and strike the weapon hand with your forearm as you do so. You should strike it so it moves toward the centerline of the assailant's body if possible. In any event, when your arm strikes his, keep it moving in an upward circular movement, lifting his shooting hand high and grabbing it with both hands in such a way as to tip the barrel straight up, then jerk it straight down, ripping it out of his hands. If for some reason you cannot rip the gun out of his hands, again, keep the barrel tipped up and away from you and start pumping those knees into his groin and lower abdomen. If you are close enough, start head-butting and biting too.

Attempted Standard Draw

If he is right-handed, put your left hand on top of his and hold the weapon in the holster. Drive your right palm

Twist, strike, and lift.

Lift the shooting hand high.

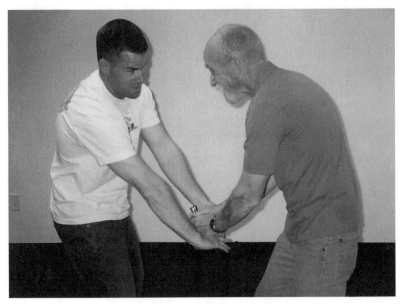

Rip the gun out of his hand.

heel up into his chin or nose. Grab the front of his shirt or thumb his eye and grab the back of his head, and then commence with the head butts and knees.

Attempted Cross Draw

If he is right-handed, put your right hand on top of his hand and your left hand on his right elbow. Knee him as you slide your left hand down his forearm between his body and the forearm. When you get both your hands on the gun, you will also have the outside of his elbow locked by the inside of your left elbow. Keep kneeing him until you can get his hands off the weapon and your right hand on it. While the pistol is still in the holster or waistband, tip the barrel toward him and pull the trigger several times. This will probably ruin his entire day.

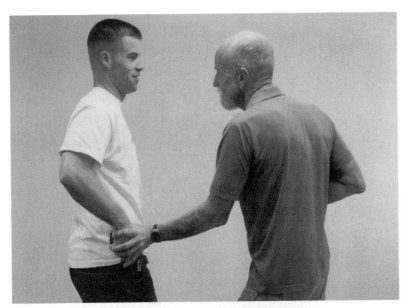

Assailant attempting a standard draw.

Hands on weapon and elbow.

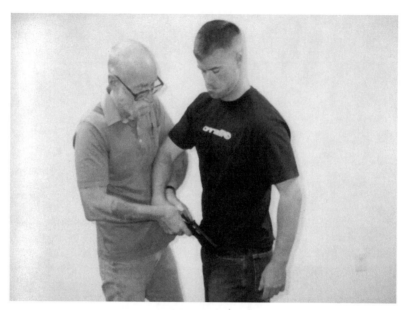

Ruining his day.

KNIVES

All we knew was that the guy had threatened the quarterdeck watch, left the ship without permission, and was on his way back to the EM Club in Pusan, Korea. Several of us left the ship to get him and bring him back before he got into more trouble. As soon as I left the prow of the ship, I could see him walking up the wharf. I headed his way at a dead run with the rest of the detail behind me. Heck, I knew the guy; I figured I would talk some sense into him and it would be over. When I got close I slowed down and yelled his name. He spun around, eyes blazing, and whipped out a watermelon knife with about a five-inch blade. I couldn't quit, couldn't let him go, and had no way of closing without getting cut. I did the only logical thing I could—I *started talking to him in a calm (yeah, sure!) voice. He began backing up, while the rest of the detail fanned out, sort of circling him, and one got behind him. As I kept chattering away, one of the other sailors did an over-arm bear hug, and the chief engineman, who was right beside me, kicked him square in the wrist, knocking the knife away and ending the affair.*

You'll hear more about this guy in the stick section.

He Has One; You Don't

Nike-do, the art of getting the you-know-what out of there, is the best means of defense when facing a knife wielder. If you have no other option but to stay and fight, face the fact that you will probably get cut, it will not hurt as badly as you think it will, and it may be life threatening without your even knowing it.

I have never used the kick to the wrist that I saw the chief do, but did see a navy shore patrolman kick a pistol out of another sailor's hand the same way (Lord knows he was lucky he didn't get shot). I practice this daily and hope I never have to use such a last-ditch move. I practice by using something that is flexible (closed-cell foam) fastened to an upright and imagine it as an arm and hand, moving around and kicking it from different directions and distances.

In a sudden blitz attack, try to get an arm up to stop the attack and simultaneously drive a punch into his head or throat with the other hand and/or grab the knife hand with both hands. Start trying to do one of two things: (1) start slamming your knee into your opponent's groin and abdomen until he goes down, or (2) start slamming his knife hand into him, a wall, a post or anything else until he drops the knife.

Practice this same set of moves against overhead stabbing attacks, upward thrusting attacks, and slashing attacks. This is a natural movement; we all have a tendency to

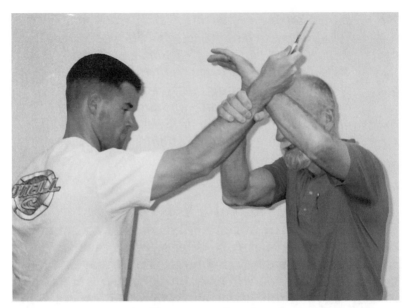

Blocking an overhead stab.

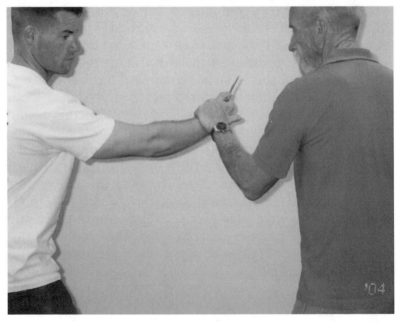

Sweeping a straight thrust.

throw up our arm to ward off a blow of any kind, and we have practiced grabbing things since we first started grabbing fingers that were held out to us when we were babies.

For a straight thrusting attack, try to deflect the attack with a sweep of your palm as you try to step out of the way, punch him, and/or then get both hands on the attacking arm/hand and start slamming him with your knees or hitting the knife hand against something.

If you have a punching bag, practice these moves standing in front of the bag, slamming it with your knees. Another helpful thing is to take a two-foot section of two-inch PVC pipe (less than $1 at most hardware stores), wrap it with one layer of closed-cell foam, duct tape the foam in place, and fill it with gravel or sand (play yard sand, not masonry sand because it has too much mica in it). Use this to represent an arm with a knife at the end of it, gripping it tightly as you slam those knees into the bag.

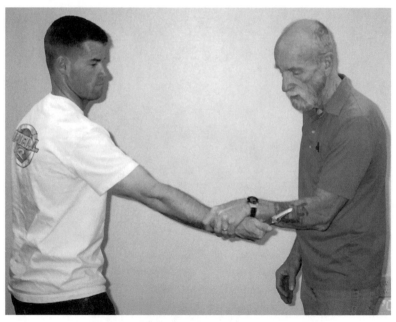

If you grab the wrist, you may get cut.

You want to try to get a grip on your opponent's hand because it gives you a little more control of the knife. The knife fighter will try to rotate his wrist and cut the arm or wrist of any hand that holds his knife arm.

Other useful defenses include wrapping your jacket around your blocking arm, throwing things, keeping a table or some other barrier between you and the knife wielder, and getting and using a weapon of your own.

Keep in mind that the guy who threatens you with a knife may or may not cut you. The guy who is really serious is probably going to keep it concealed until he starts sticking and cutting on you. At that point you are in deep trouble.

You Have One; He Doesn't

I do recommend that women joggers—or anyone who has to walk or jog alone in a rural area or anyplace there is a likelihood of being attacked without warning—carry a

The jacket wrap.

Jacket wrap and grab.

weapon. Predators (cougars and thugs) are especially prone to attacking women joggers without warning. I suggest carrying a small knife with locking blade that has a thumbhole or stud to facilitate one-hand opening and a small lanyard. You should carry this knife in your hand and loop the lanyard over your wrist or little finger so it won't fly out of your hand if you are suddenly grabbed or thrown to the ground. In this scenario, there is no time to get a knife out of a sheath or pocket that you may be lying on. Use that thumbhole to pop out the blade, and start stabbing and cutting.

You should *never* brandish a knife to warn or threaten anyone; this establishes intent to do great bodily harm. If, on the other hand, you whip the knife out and start stabbing, you may be able to justify self-defense. Never try to use a knife without realizing that it could result in the attacker's death and/or prison time for you. If you cannot

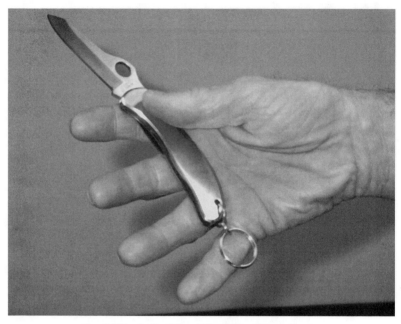

Lock-blade knife with little finger loop.

control your emotions well enough to be able to depend on your always making a rational decision about the use of a knife, *don't carry one, ever,* and don't even go near one when you are upset.

If you must use a knife to protect yourself from harm, here are a few pointers.

- Use a lanyard if possible. You are going to get banged around, your hand is going to get wet, and the knife will be slippery; once you get started you don't want to lose it. Things are going to get pretty confused, and you may even cut yourself in the melee.
- Get a death grip on that knife. Keep the blade pointed out of the thumb side of your fist.
- Try to maintain a mobile stance, much like that of a boxer, but with the following exceptions:

- Keep your empty hand up in front of and close to the area from the center of your chest to your lower throat. Use that hand to block and grab.
- If your opponent is unarmed, keep the blade low and semiconcealed near your thigh. Maintain a left-side lead (if you are right-handed). When you close the distance between you and your opponent, grab his head or clothing with your left hand and start stabbing upward into his thighs, groin, and lower abdomen. Don't stop until he starts to go down, then hit his neck. This is virtually an assassination and should not be done unless there is no other way to preserve your own life or someone else's.

You attack with a knife.

Stab to the lower body.

- If your opponent is armed, adopt a right-side lead with your RIGHT hand held a bit higher than your left and about four inches in front of your body. Try to meet any move he makes with a cut to the extended limb, a grab, or at least a push of the extended limb with your empty hand and a quick stab to his neck, face, or upper body.
- If he grabs your knife hand, rotate your wrist and use your knife to cut his arm.
- Carve from wood a dull version of the knife you usually carry and use that for practice. What is the sense of practicing with a Bowie when you carry a Swiss army knife?

Leading with the knife hand.

Stabbing the face or neck.

I have never been involved in a knife-to-knife fight, but my mom told me of one that she witnessed, and it illustrates the utter foolishness of thinking you are going to come out unscathed in a knife fight She watched two women go at it, one slashing with a butcher knife and the other stabbing with an ice pick. The butcher knife was held like a hammer, and the ice pick like (duh) an ice pick. There was a lot of slashing and stabbing, but once the ice pick went into the chest it was all over. I don't think there is really any safe way to face a knife, unless you have about 40 feet of distance and a 12-gauge shotgun.

WEAPONS AT HAND

We were hanging out in a junkyard in Birmingham, Alabama. It was a rough part of town, and every one of us had been in some sort of brawl in the near vicinity. The back gate to the junkyard was open, as was the roll-up door to the shop. Across one side of the shop ran a long workbench that had tools scattered along its length. We were warming up by the stove, smoking, and telling lies, when we heard a commotion and two men came running through the back gate toward the shop. The one in the lead was unarmed, but his pursuer had what appeared to be a four-inch steak knife. They came into the shop at a dead run, and as the lead man passed the workbench he picked up two ball-peen hammers, slid to a stop, and faced Mr. Knifer. They only paused for a split second, and the roles changed, Mr. Knifer spun and left at a dead run with the hammer man close on his heels. With true Southern humor, one of the guys by the stove said laconically, "Gentlemen, you have just seen the world's fastest hammer thief."

Everything around you can be used as a weapon. Fire extinguishers, aerosol cans, spray bottles—anything that will squirt works wonders. Anything you can pick up is a bludgeon, and anything with a point can be used as a strike enhancer or a stabbing utensil. The nunchackus, tonfas, and sais of Oriental martial arts were at one time common tools of that culture and were developed into awesome weapons. If you don't have those at hand, there is an endless variety of implements all around you that can be used to distract and/or injure anyone who attacks you.

Short Stick
(Or Any Number of Suitable Substitutes)

Remember the knifer in Pusan? Well, we thought the problem had been resolved and we could go back to watching the ship's evening movie. Suddenly, he burst from behind the movie screen swinging a two-foot pipe wrench. I was in the front row, right in front of him, and there was nowhere to run because of the sailors around me. Without thinking, I simply attacked him. I sprang up from the bench I was sitting on, wrapped both arms around his upper body, hooked my right leg around his left one, and pushed. We went down with me on top, and he lost the wrench. The chief engineman I mentioned earlier took the guy down to the engine room and, with help from some of his engineers, tied him up like a mummy. He didn't cause any more trouble that night, and as best as I remember, he got three months in the brig for the evening's escapade.

Defending against a stick is not a piece of cake but is considerably safer that defending against a knife because it doesn't cut as well. On the other hand, a stick can kill, too; it just takes a bit more deliberate intent to do it. What you want to do is avoid the last four inches of the tip of the

Block the stick.

stick. This means staying outside the range of the stick until you can time a rush to close the gap with the stick swinger. When you do make the rush, you need to try to do four things almost simultaneously:

1) Block his weapon arm by striking somewhere near his elbow with your forearm held at about a 90-degree angle to his striking arm.

Grab and hang on.

2) Grab him, either at the front of his shirt or by his hair, the nape of his neck, or the back of his head, and hang on.

Knee the groin.

3) Start slamming in those knees to the groin and abdomen, and add a few head butts to flavor the sauce.

Wrap the attacking arm and disarm.

4) Let your blocking arm slide over and wrap around the arm it just blocked, and then jerk your fist up near your ear. Normally, the stick will go flying, or you will catch it and now have it as a weapon, or you will at least have immobilized his striking arm while you knee and head-butt him into damaged goods.

A swing to your leg is going to be extremely painful, but you can survive it. The best solution is to charge in and jam the swing, and then get right with the dirty stuff.

The Filipino martial arts are excellent sources of training for knife and stick fighting (as well as striking and grappling). I don't propose to teach anywhere near all of the nuances of this superb fighting art, but here are a few ideas on stick fighting.

- Train with a stick of the length you are likely to use. I use a 20-inch stick because that is the length of the handle on the windshield washer squeegee that I keep in my truck. Filipino martial artists typically train with sticks 27 inches or longer.
- Adopt a sort of a boxer's stance but with a right-hand, right-foot lead (if you are right-handed), keep your empty hand up about in front of and close to the area from the center of your chest to your lower throat. Use this hand, referred to as the "live hand," to parry, block, and grab, also known as "checking."
- Most of your strikes are going to be made on a downward stroke of 45 degrees, and virtually all the rest will either be vertical or horizontal to the ground. Fasten something flexible (I use closed-cell foam) to an upright and imagine it's an arm and hand. Move around, striking it from different directions and distances. You are practicing hitting the opponent's hand, in what Filipino martial artists refer to as "defanging the snake." That is a good analogy. If you hit the hand, you end the threat of any weapon it held and may well end the fight itself. Don't stop here, though; use a heavy bag or whatever you have rigged up to practice strikes to the face, neck, thighs, and groin.
- Try to imagine which directions an attack would come from and use the stick to deflect or stop them.
- Practice these techniques on a punching bag, in empty air, or with a partner (go slow with a partner and use padded sticks and hand and head protection).

Cane

I was in a train station in Tokyo, rushing to catch a train, when I saw a U.S. Air Force sergeant step on the foot of an elderly Japanese man who was carrying a cane. The elderly man stepped back, smiled, and nodded that all was OK. For some reason, the idiotic sergeant then deliberately stepped on the man's foot again. I headed that way because I detest bullies and was anticipating putting a stop to that nonsense. Then I stopped to enjoy the show. The old gentleman's cane turned into a blur as he glided around driving two-handed strikes into the bully's shins, ankles, and calves. Almost immediately, the sergeant was on the deck and the old man just disappeared into the crowd.

Upward whip to hand.

You can carry a walking cane almost anywhere, even aboard an airliner, and no one is going to stop you because it is legal everywhere. This is especially true if you are older or have a back problem (or even think you might). I recommend getting one that is substantial, such as the cattle or hog canes sold in many ranch supply stores or one of the custom-made fighting canes advertised in martial arts magazines. The lightweight ones won't hold up very well with the power you can generate with both hands on the stick. I recommend practicing, at the very least, the following techniques:

- When you are standing naturally with the cane in your hand, its tip on the ground, practice whipping it upward into a hand (foam cylinder fastened to an upright). Also practice whipping it up into the groin of

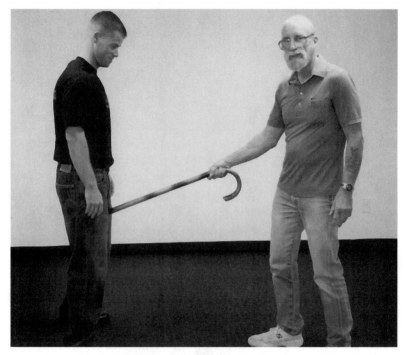

Upward whip to groin.

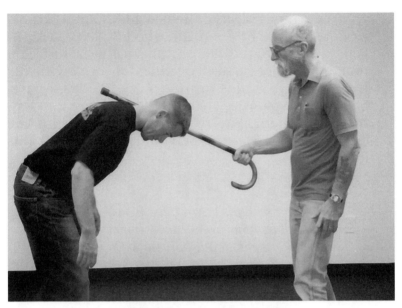

Follow-up swing downward.

Baseball-type swing to legs.

an opponent (better use a homemade dummy of some kind, unless you have a friend who just loves pain).

- Follow each upward whip by delivering a sort of a roundhouse, one-handed, overhand swing downward.
- Now get both hands on that stick like it's a baseball bat and practice striking the forearms and legs of an opponent. You really don't want to hit the head or neck area because you could kill with this much power.

Chair

This particular Alabama roadhouse was one of those places that would serve almost anyone who could belly up to the bar, and belly up I did. I was sitting there at the age of 16, hoisting a few "adult beverages" and shooting the breeze with a friend, when a commotion started between the bartender and another customer at the far end of the bar. Suddenly, the customer jumped over the bar and took the bartender down as he did. Then they were on the floor behind the bar, and the customer was on top of the bartender pelting a steady rain of punches into his face. I, the shameless spectator, leaned over the bar to get a better look. I was totally focused on the show and never saw the chair that someone slammed into my back as I leaned over the bar. Trust me, this was a better quality chair than you see in the movies; it didn't shatter, but I almost did. My friend dragged me out of the joint, threw me into the car, and got the heck out of there as the rest of the place exploded into a wild free-for-all.

A chair is a heck of a weapon, whether you swing it or jab with it. Frankly, I have seen it thrown more than swung or jabbed. The best thing you can do with it is throw it through a window and then follow it through as you get the heck out of Dodge.

Pen

Never be without a click-type ballpoint pen in your shirt pocket. Whether grappling on the ground or standing, you can quickly bring it into play as a stabbing instrument. Drive it down into the hands of someone who has you in a rear bear hug with your arms outside. Drive it up into the elbow or arm when you are caught in a rear naked choke. If you are really desperate, you can drive it into an attacker's eye or throat.

Keys

Carry your keys on a ring attached to a metal snap swivel. You can hook the snap swivel onto your belt loop, and the keys are always readily accessible. Always have your keys in your hand when you go to your car or door;

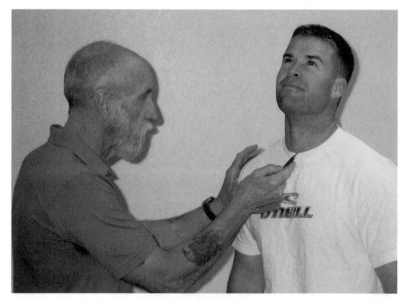

Pen to throat.

Key ring rigging.

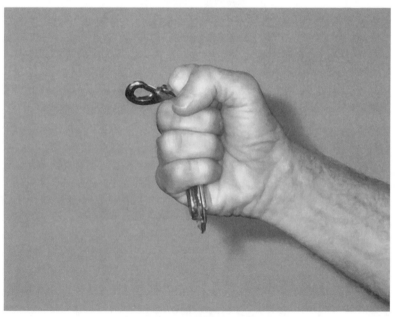

Strike with the key ring.

don't wait and then fumble with your stuff after you get there. Practice taking your keys off your belt loop in such a way that the snap part of the snap swivel naturally protrudes between your middle and index fingers and the keys protrude from the bottom of your fist. This is one heck of a strike enhancer, whether you strike with the fist or bottom fist. Simply raking the keys sharply across an attacker's forehead will bring blood.

Screwdriver

The screwdriver is almost as good as a knife—in some ways even better. The screwdriver requires a powerful hit to penetrate and, since it is dull, hurts a lot worse than a knife. You can't slash with it like you can a knife, but you do have plausible deniability when it comes time for the trial. You weren't intending to go armed; you just happened to have a common tool at hand.

The windshield washer.

Windshield Washer

For some weapons with excellent plausible deniability, try keeping a bottle of glass cleaner and a window washer/squeegee in your car. Get the kind that is made of a hard, flexible plastic and has a screw-off squeegee head. The glass cleaner will sting an attacker's eyes at close range, and the handle minus the squeegee head makes a great little fighting stick. Everyone needs these in the car anyway to clean the road film off the windows on a regular basis for driving safety.

Cars

Pop was driving along a deserted road near El Dorado, Arkansas, when he saw a coatless man hitchhiking along the side of the road. It was cold, and Pop thought he would help the guy out. He stopped and picked him up, but right away he got a feeling that something was wrong. Then the guy asked him to stop in a swampy area that was especially desolate. When Pop refused, the man insisted. Pop floored the Ford and took Mister Hitchhiker on the ride of his life. The man had both hands on the seat of the car and was begging Pop to slow down, but he kept pouring on the coal until they came into the next town, where he slid to a stop right in front of the police station. Pop went out his door, and the hitchhiker went out of the other one at a dead run.

Don't pick up hitchhikers, and don't hitchhike; it is dangerous both ways. As soon as you get in your car, lock the doors, start the engine, put it in gear, and release the emergency brake. If anyone comes up to the car and is the least bit threatening, don't hesitate—release the foot brake and accelerate. A shooter probably won't be able to hit you when you are moving, and no one else is going to be able to get to you. You are driving a 4,000-pound bullet. Don't worry about getting in a wreck or hurting someone; you can work that out later. What you want to do is survive. When you stop in traffic, always stop so you can see the bottom of the tires of the car in front of you. At this distance you can cut your wheels and go around without having to back up to gain driving room. This is a good defense against carjackings.

Stationary Weapons

The first time I saw a big mailbox used as a weapon I was amazed. The winner of the fight got his opponent in a headlock and then ran him into the mailbox. Then he repeated it twice more before the cops came and broke it up. The loser was bleeding like a stuck hog but was still conscious; I guess he had a thick head.

I have circled around pillars and such to keep me clear of an attacker until I could recover long enough to get back into the game. I have also pushed a guy's head down, grabbed the seat of his baggy britches, and run him into a wall. Look for ways to use your environment, such as slamming a guy's head against the ground when you are in the mounted position.

YOUR MIND

Your mind is the very best weapon you have available. Put it to work right now and figure out what you can use and how.

Chapter 7

Physical Training

"The more you sweat in training, the less you'll bleed in battle." I've heard that mantra ever since I joined the navy in 1956.

There is no end to the reasons we need to be in good physical condition, and not just for fighting. If you want to do anything other than be a couch potato, you can do it better if you are in good physical shape. Almost every one of the street fighters I have known has done conditioning of some kind. Many did hard manual labor, working as butchers, warehouse men, loggers, carpenters, and so on. In addition to training in their own personal fighting styles or techniques, many of those hard-working guys also trained with weights, calisthenics, cables, or odd objects.

Physical training also trains your mind. It develops the grit to go ahead and complete that last rep, to run one more wind sprint, to go one more round on the heavy bag. It also inures you to pain to some degree. That last push-up hurts, running the final mile hurts, sparring another round hurts, and you learn that you can endure pain and overcome the obstacle in front of

119

you. If you allow yourself to quit when things become inconvenient or uncomfortable, you are not training yourself to win; you are training yourself to lose.

I do not hold myself up as an expert in physical conditioning by any means—one look at my skinny body will quickly convince you of that. On the other hand, I am a distance hiker who often rock climbs, mountain bikes, cuts and splits wood, shovels snow, and does it all past the ripe old age of 60. Endurance sports have long been a source of enjoyment to me, and the way I train reflects what I enjoy.

Everyone has specific ideas about how folks ought to train, and some people are pretty adamant about it. There are certified experts who say you should do the same workout every other day, or every day, or work certain muscle groups only once or sometimes twice a week. There are just as many varying opinions on stretching, diet, aerobics, plyometrics, and just about every other facet of physical training. My advice to you is to learn as much as you can about training and try a great variety of things, then do what is right for you at the time. I find that my training varies from day to day, depending on what I have just read/heard about and how I am feeling at the time. A bit later on I will outline my basic workout program and go into detail on the exercises, but first I want to mention weight training.

I think lifting weights is a good thing, and though I don't often train with weights and frankly know little about them, I would like to make a few observations based on what I have been told by folks who do:

1) If you are going to train with weights, get some guidance from a trainer or experienced lifter. Some lifts can be damaging to your back and joints if done improperly.
2) Build your workout around the basic compound joint movements, such as squats, dead lifts, power cleans, push presses, and pull-ups.
3) Training with odd objects can be a good thing; use

sandbags, kegs, or logs. Do a bit of sled or car pushing and some tire tossing. These things build real, functional strength.

4) Don't forget to add in some aerobic training.

This is my standard system of training. It won't make you big and buff, but last summer (my 60th) I did 22 dead-hang pull-ups and hiked the 22-mile Mount Whitney (California) Trail in one day. Although I didn't get into any brawl, I did stand beside a bear box in the campground and threaten to kick a bear's butt. The bear finally decided to leave this crazy man's lunch alone. Like everything else in this guide, nothing here is carved in stone. Take it and customize it to fit your needs.

LOOSENING UP

Most of these exercises I learned in 1963 from a Shotokan karate instructor named James Arwood. The reason for doing them is to warm up and get the juices flowing to your joints when you first get up and before you exercise if you have been inactive for any period of time. Do 5 or 10 in each direction of swing or rotation. Don't try to go as far as you can, just to the point of being slightly stretched but still comfortable. The loosening-up exercises can all be done from the standing position.

Neck
- Nod your chin down to your chest and then tip your head toward your back.
- Lean your ear down toward your shoulder and then toward the other one.
- Look first to one side and then to the other.

Arms and Shoulders
- With your elbows at your sides, make circles in each direction with your hands.

- Same position, make circles with your forearms.
- Rotate your shoulders in both directions.
- Extend your arms out to the side and rotate them in small circles.
- Now swing your arms horizontally across your chest and back out.
- Put one hand above your head and the other at your side, and swing them vertically.

The following is an excellent rotator cuff exercise (do 3 sets of 10 as part of the warmup):

- Fasten a length of surgical tubing or other elastic material to a doorknob, vice, or whatever is at about elbow height.
- Stand with your side toward the vice (or whatever) with your upper arm alongside your body and your elbow bent so that your forearm is at a 90-degree angle to your upper arm. Now pull the tubing across your body, moving only your lower arm.
- Now reverse your position so that you pull the tubing in the opposite direction.
- Hold two small weights or cans of beans, etc. (never exceed five pounds with this exercise). Stand erect and raise your arms in a sort of "I surrender" position, elbows bent at about 90 degrees, upper arms parallel to the floor. Now lower your forearms so the weights are pointed at the floor, and then raise them to the original position.

Ankles and Knees

- Extend your foot slightly in front of you and rotate your foot.
- Put your hands on your hips, feet together; squat very slightly and rotate your knees.

Waist
Put your hands on your hips and swing your hips in a circle.

CIRCUIT TRAINING

I usually work out every day but Sunday. I do what I refer to as the personalized combat form (see the next chapter) nonstop for 45 minutes to an hour on Monday, Wednesday, and Friday. I normally do circuit training on Tuesday, Thursday, and Saturday because I enjoy working out nonstop and believe that I get an aerobic workout as well as a resistance workout with circuit training. I usually do 5 to 10 circuits, taking the exercises almost to failure or to some predetermined number. I vary my workout regularly, but what follows is the circuit that I base it on.

- Street fighter squats
- Pull-ups
- Stick or grippers
- Push-ups
- Crunches
- Hyperextensions or Upas

Street Fighter Squats
Start off standing erect with your feet about six to eight inches apart and your hands extended in front of you. Draw your hands back to your chest as you inhale. Drop your hands straight down at your sides as you simultaneously exhale and lower yourself until your thighs are parallel to the floor and you have raised your heels up off of the floor. Now stand up and raise your hands straight in front of you as your feet return to being flat on the floor and you are in the starting position. This is one repetition. Start with 10 or 20 reps and work up. This variation on the standard squat is particularly beneficial training for street fighting because you come up on your toes, which exercises your calves and ankles as well as your balance.

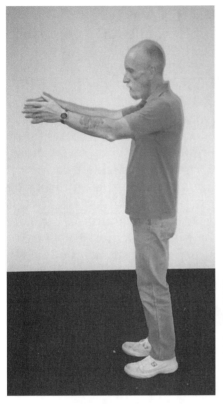

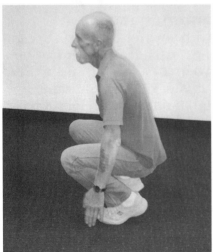

*Stand erect with arms
extended in front (above
left).*

*Inhale and draw your
hands in toward your
chest (above).*

*Lower into a street fighter
squat—thighs parallel to
the floor, heels up (left).*

Pull-Ups

I use a pull-up bar made of pipe and some braces I bought in a hardware store. The braces are mounted above a doorway in my workshop/gym, and the pipe is held in place with hose clamps. Either stand on something or give a little jump; grab the bar with both hands, palms facing away from you; and hang at full arm extension. Now pull yourself up until your chin goes over the bar, and then lower yourself to full arm extension again. This is one repetition of a standard pull-up. I mostly do parallel pull-ups using this bar and some homemade handles that attach to the bar about shoulder width apart and allow me to do pull-ups with my palms facing each other. I believe that having your palms facing each other during most exercises places less stress on your vulnerable shoulder joints. You can achieve pretty much the same effect without the handles by doing commando pull-ups, standing under the bar and grasping it from opposite sides You are now standing perpendicular to the bar. Now pull up, with your head first on one side of the bar and then on the other.

If you do not have a pull-up bar or are unable to complete a pull-up, there are some variations that might work for you. Do the same thing but use a walking cane or stick to do the pulling movement. Place the stick across the backs of two chairs and do a sort of supine row: Lie on your back on the floor with your upper body between the two chairs and your hands extended straight up, grasping the stick. Now keep your body straight and use your arms to pull your chest toward the bar. Only your heels should be touching the floor when doing the exercise. Do this slowly, and don't "drop" back to the extended position because it seems to stress the joints. You can also hook the crook of the walking cane over a tree branch, rafter, or pipe and, holding on to the shaft, do pull-ups that are much like climbing a rope.

If you have a pull-up bar, some playground equipment, or even a tree limb, here are a few more varieties of this excellent exercise:

- *Negatives*—Stand on a chair or such, placing yourself in the "up" position, and then step off and slowly lower yourself to the full dead-hang position
- *Sternum pull-ups*—Pull yourself up until your sternum touches the bar.
- *Side-to-side pull-ups*—Swing to first one side and then the other as you do pull-ups, thereby putting more stress on the arm that is on the side you are swinging to.
- *Chin-ups*—Chin-ups are done like a pull-upp but with your palms facing toward you. Hang a rope from your bar and do these with one hand on the rope and one hand on the bar.
- *Towel pull-ups*—Hang a towel over the bar and hold on to it as you do pull-ups.
- *Fence post pull-ups*—Use a four-inch fence post nailed up between two trees to do pull-ups, which is a major grip workout as well.

If you work out at home and then go to a park or some other place to do your pull-ups, the following gymnast regimen is a good pull-up-only workout:

1) Wide-grip pull-ups to failure. Rest 10 seconds.
2) Medium-grip pull-ups to failure. Rest 10 seconds.
3) Medium grip chin-ups (palms facing you) to failure. Rest 10 seconds.
4) Close-grip chin-ups to failure.
5) Commando pull-ups to failure. Rest 3 minutes.
6) Do the whole thing over again twice more.

By now you may have gotten the idea that I am highly in favor of pull-ups.

Stick

Hold a stick (a walking cane works well) in both hands. Squeeze it with one hand and twist it with the other. Twist it in both directions. This gives your hands and forearms a good workout, much like using a screwdriver on a stubborn screw.

Grippers

I use grippers from Ironmind (www.ironmind.com), and they are excellent. When you work up to about 10 to 12 repetitions on a gripper, it is about time to start training with the next harder one. Start with a trainer model or, if you already have a really good grip, a #1. Ironmind also sells a lot of other really great weight and grip training equipment, as well as some excellent books.

Push-Ups

Standard push-up position—toes and palms on the floor, arms extended and about shoulder width apart, back straight. Lower yourself until your chest almost touches the floor, and then push yourself up to the starting position. Variations include very slow negatives, claps between reps, one-handed push-ups, and diamond push-ups (triceps). You can also do them with push-up bars, with a backpack on, with one hand on a concrete block, with your feet on a chair, with one foot resting on the other ankle, and so on. I find it helps to inhale as you lower yourself and to slightly purse your lips and breathe out explosively as you push up. If you are unable to do a push-up, build up to it by assuming the push-up position and then slowly lowering yourself until you are flat on the floor. An easier option is to rest on your knees instead of your toes and do the push-ups from that position. I typically use a homemade set of push-up bars to do these because I believe that having your palms facing each other during most exercises places less stress on your vulnerable shoulder joints.

Crunches

For standard crunches, lie supine on the mat with your knees bent and your feet flat. Hold your fists alongside your face but not supporting or pulling on your head. Imagine you are balancing a glass of water on your forehead as you attempt to draw your ribcage toward your pelvis. Hold each crunch a second or two.

Hyperextensions

Lie in the prone position with your face flat on the floor and your hands alongside your thighs but not touching the floor. Now, raise both your legs and upper body so that only your belly is touching the floor. Relax and repeat. Try to work up to a total of about 100 during the course of your workout.

Upas

Lie supine on the mat, knees bent, feet on the floor, as if you were about to do crunches. Raise your hips until your thighs and body form a straight line and only your feet and shoulders are touching the floor.

NECK WORK

Neck work should be done after you complete the circuit training above. Use your hand(s) on the front, side, and back of your head to provide resistance as you move your head through the full range of motion, forward, to each side, and to the back, You can do this in either the standing or sitting position. Do three to five sets of ten repetitions here.

STRETCHING

The purpose of stretching is to stretch the muscle, increase blood flow to the area, and hopefully prevent injury. When stretching, you should feel the stretch in the muscle—never in the joint. Only stretch to the point of slight discomfort, never to the feeling of pain. Hold each stretch for 20 to 30 seconds.

Calf

Stand with your feet about eight inches apart. Move your right foot about two and a half feet to the rear, and keep the soles of both feet on the floor. Now sort of lower yourself by bending your knee and lunging forward a bit, and you should feel the stretch in your right calf. Now stretch the other calf.

Quadriceps

Stand up and hold on to something with your left hand for support, bend your right knee, grasp your instep with your right hand, and pull your foot up toward your butt. You should feel the stretch in your quadriceps. Now stretch the other leg.

Relax

Lie in the prone position with your hands at your sides and your head turned to one side for three minutes. Relax and empty your mind.

Sphinx

From the above position push yourself up to a position where you are resting on your elbows and your back is arched. Relax and empty your mind for three minutes.

Cobra

Lie face down on the mat. Use your arms to push your upper body upward while leaving your hips on the mat. Try to get your arms to full extension. You should feel this stretch in your lower and middle back. Hold yourself at full extension for a second or two, and then lower down, resume the facedown position on the mat, and relax for a few seconds. Repeat for a total of 10 extensions.

Hamstrings

Lie supine with one leg extended on the floor and the other up and almost perpendicular to your body. Hook a belt, towel, or the crook of a walking cane over the instep of that perpendicular leg and pull it toward your head once you are able to straighten it. You should feel the tightness in your hamstring. Hold it for 20 to 30 seconds and then switch to the other leg.

THE FINAL EXERCISES

When I have the space and equipment at hand, I usually finish off my workout with the following exercises:

Jump Rope

Get a good-quality jump rope with a leather cord and ball bearings in the handles. Adjust it so that if you stand on it with your feet about 12 inches apart the point where the rope joins the handles will come about two inches above your hip bones. Use a jump rope mat or other padded surface. Start with the rope touching the floor behind you, swing it over your head, and hop over it as it comes by. Start out at a speed that feels right for you, and gradually try to work up to a speed of about 120 to 150 jumps per minute. This is just a starter; eventually you will be skipping the rope, jumping first on one foot and then the other, and other variations. Start off doing only one three-minute round of this exercise and then work up to doing several rounds with a one-minute rest in between. When you have been doing five three-minute rounds for a while, you can lengthen the rounds and eventually work up to one fifteen-minute round. This is a great calf builder, as well as a great footwork developer. It is also a good cardiovascular workout. For more detailed information on this great exercise, read *MAX O2: The Complete Guide to Synergistic Aerobic Training* by Jerry Robinson and Frank Carrino.

Speed Bag

Boxers and other martial artists use the speed bag because it develops speed, rhythm, and hand-eye coordination and gets you used to seeing leather flying near your face. It does not really duplicate any specific punches. It is also, quite simply, a fun exercise. I use it as a warm-down after my workout as well as before stretching, doing three rounds with no break.

Adjust the bag so that the largest part of it is about on level with a spot between your nose and upper lip. Remember to keep your elbows up when striking. After the first hit, start striking the bag just as it rebounds from the far side of the drum (the round piece it hangs from). Your punch should strike the part of the bag that tapers up to the swivel just above the largest part of the bag. Do not try to hit hard or fast; work at controlling the bag. Speed will come; save the power for the heavy bag and the ring.

Start off striking with one hand, hitting it with the bottom of your fist (remember to keep your elbow up). Your hand should be going in a circular motion as you strike. Count as you hear the drumbeats: (1) should be your fist and the first time it hits the far side of the drum, (2) should be when it hits the drum right in front of your face, and (3) should be as it hits the far side of the drum again. Keep counting and hitting 1, 2, 3 for a minute or so. Next shift to your other hand and do the same with that hand for a while. Finally, start to hit first with the bottom of your fist and then the fore knuckles of the opposite hand, almost like you are throwing an overhand right (remember, keep your elbows up when striking the speed bag). Follow that fore-knuckle punch with a bottom fist strike of the same hand. Maintain the same 1, 2, 3 rhythm the whole time.

With a bit of practice (about 15 minutes or so), you should be hitting the speed bag with a fairly decent rhythm, using alternate hands to first strike fore knuckle and then bottom fist with first one hand and then the other.

Heavy Bag

There is always controversy about how to hit the heavy bag. Opinions are like armpits; everyone has a couple, and a lot of them stink. I'm sure some experts out there will think mine do.

• The heavy bag trains you to hit harder with your fists.

- Always wear heavy (12- or 16-oz.) gloves when you hit the heavy bag.
- Only hit the heavy bag once a week.
- Use it to develop each punch individually.
- Gradually start working it with combinations of punches that you feel you have a sound basis in.
- Almost everyone will tell you to work it in three-minute rounds because boxers do. I recommend working the heavy bag with everything from three- to fifteen-minute rounds.

That is the workout. Give it all you have got, and it will definitely pay off for you. Yes, it does take a good bit of time to do all of this. I generally spend one to one and a half hours each morning working out. I also slack off at times and only do part of the workout. Go with what your body tells you to do.

Chapter 8

Personalized Combat Form

n the early seventies I was mostly practicing judo and shotokan. I enjoyed doing the katas of shotokan, but they didn't seem to be practical training for close-quarter combat (at least for me). Browsing in a bookstore one day, I came across a book on t'ai-chi chu'an (taijiquan), and the flyleaf explained that the one kata-like form of ta'i-chi provided everything that one needed to practice to be competent in self-defense. The idea of one formal exercise that provided a single means of practicing the most important parts of a hand-to-hand combat system really intrigued me and inspired me to work on developing such an exercise. I tried combining the parts of the katas I knew to develop this ultimate kata. As time went on, I began adding and dropping techniques to give me practice in the ones that seemed most applicable to my needs.

The pattern of techniques, or personalized combat form (PCF), that I developed over a number of years simply consists of the ambidextrous practice of close-quarter combat techniques that have proved useful to me in the past. When done at average speed, the whole thing can be completed in about 10 minutes. I believe each person should develop his or her own pattern and do it daily. Doing so will help you to develop muscle memory as you practice the techniques that you want to become as natural as walking. Include all the heel tactics that you seldom practice, such as biting, foot stomps, head butts, and so forth. I use a double-double end bag I bought from Ringside (www.ringside.com). The bag is attached at the top to the top of a doorway and at the bottom by two bungee cords that go to each side of the lower part of the doorway. At the levels that would be the crotch and throat on a human opponent, I have padded the bag with closed-cell foam so I can strike and grasp these areas. Screwed into the floor in the center of the doorway is a shoe that I use for stomping on when I practice clinching. For the ground grappling part of the form, I use a grappling dummy that is made from stacks of newspaper and has a soccer ball for a head. It even has a neck made of a roll of newspaper. The whole thing is held together by duct tape and weighs about 65 pounds.

I also perform the PCF at normal speed using no accoutrements whatsoever, much like the forms that are practiced in many of the Oriental martial arts. When you first start developing your own PCF or following the one outlined in this chapter, it is helpful to post the list of techniques in a readable position somewhere in your training area, do the movements slowly, and make sure that you are able to keep your balance at all times. It will take a while to get it all down, but eventually you'll be able to do it at full speed and full power with or without training apparatus. This is in itself a good aerobic workout if repeated a few times.

As you perform your PCF, there is one overriding principle you should bear in mind, and it is the most important one in this book: *You will do what you train to do.* If you train to pull your punches, you will pull your punches when you need them most; don't pull your punches in training. If you fold when hurt, that is what you will do in combat; if you get hurt in training, get mad. If you train 15 different ways of breaking a hand grab, you will hesitate and think when someone grabs your wrist; learn as few techniques as possible and master them.

The informal outline below is mostly a list of the situations that you would be wise to be prepared for. I recommend that you use it as a general guide to develop your own PCF. All of the techniques listed in the PCF outlined here were described and explained in detail in the preceding chapters. As we have seen, often the same techniques are useful in a variety of situations.

Note that the PCF presented here deals with weapons first. This is because an armed opponent is probably the most dangerous threat you will face. You need to know how to use and defend against weapons.

1. **You Are Armed**
   A. Knife
      1. Defend against a knife
      2. Attack an unarmed assailant in self-defense
   B. Short stick
      1. Strike opponent's hands
      2. Strike opponent's face, groin, and legs
   C. Walking cane
      1. Upward whip to opponent's hand
      2. Upward whip to opponent's groin
      3. Two-handed blows to opponent's forearms and legs

2. **Opponent Is Armed**
   A. Handgun disarms
      1. Gun pointed at you from a distance
      2. Gun held to your head
      3. Gun held to your abdomen
      4. Gun held to your back
      5. Attempted straight draw
      6. Attempted cross draw

B. Knife disarms
   1. Downward stab
   2. Slash from the side
   3. Upward stab
   4. Straight thrust
C. Stick disarms
   1. Downward swing
   2. Diagonal downward swing
   3. Horizontal swing

3. **You Are Both Unarmed**
   A. Breakaways
      1. Wrist grabs
      2. Lapel grabs
      3. Rear shoulder grabs
      4. Full nelson
      5. Headlock
      6. Rear naked choke
      7. Bear hug
      8. Hammer lock
   B. Defenses against blows and throws
      1. Takedowns
         a. Snapdown and kick
         b. Sprawl
      2. Kicks
         a. Scoop block and dive
         b. Shin block and punches
         c. Elbow clamp and forearm block
      3. Punches
         a. Parry and grab
         b. slip and bob
         c. dive, grab, and knee and/or head-butt
   C. Preemptive attacks
      1. Front kick to groin
      2. Dive in, grab, and knee and/or head-butt
      3. Palm heel thrust
      4. Head butt
      5. Front kick and/or dive

D. Ground grappling
1. You are in his guard
2. You have mounted
3. You are in his mount
4. He is in your guard
5. Rock and roll to kick standing opponent
6. Cross ankle lock his rear scissors
7. Breaking headlocks
8. Getting to your feet

This will not cover every conceivable situation you might encounter, but it will sure cover most of them. You may have techniques or situations that you like better than those listed here; use what is right for you.

Epilogue

his is the end. It has been short and sweet. Read it over several times. There is a lot of truth here and not a lot of bovine excrement trying to sell my ideas. Following are some of the most important concepts I've covered:

- You will do what you train to do.
- Develop your own personalized combat form and practice it daily.
- Always be aware of your surroundings.
- If your instinct tells you something is awry, get out of there fast; your subconscious is smarter than you are. Do not be afraid to be inconvenienced.
- Sprinting is almost always a good option.
- Do not comply with verbal orders from an attacker; he wants to move you to a secure location so he can do what he wants without being interrupted.